Advance Praise for

The New Sustainability Advantage

This book is an invaluable read for sustainability insiders as well as
first timers. The structure of *The New Sustainability Advantage* is so well
thought through that it allows the reader to get the information they need
quickly and efficiently. Beyond the impressive data and logic of the business
case for sustainability, the real lessons lie in the humility, creativity, persistence
and passion for which Willard has become internationally renowned.

—Dr. James Gray-Donald, Associate Vice-President, Sustainability Leader,
Sears Canada Inc.

In his book, *The New Sustainability Advantage*, Bob Willard articulates
the business case for sustainability and the alignment of the for-profit
mandate with the pursuit of environmental and social benefits.
Using examples, he demonstrates that sustainability is a material source of
business value when employed as a strategic framework for innovation, value
creation, and organizational enhancement. Milton Friedman's edict — that
the business of business is business, and the creation of shareholder profit
is its fundamental mandate — is just as true now as it ever was. Yet — as the
reader discovers — what has changed is the context within which business
operates, and thus how one bounds this edict in the pursuit of sustainable
capitalism. The sources of value available to business and the competitive
forces acting upon it are dynamic. We should not be surprised by shifts
in business criteria, sources of value, or changes in the business
activities required delivering a winning value proposition.

—Tyler J. Elm, Vice President, Business Sustainability,
Canadian Tire Corporation

Through his new book, Bob gives us a more compelling business case for
sustainable practices that help the bottom line by capitalizing on employees'
emotional engagement and culture change. His business case for investing
in sustainability strategies is realistic, achievable, and profitable.

—Claude Ouimet, Senior V.P. General Manager for Canada and Latin America
at InterfaceFLOR

10 years after publishing his ground-breaking book, Bob Willard
continues his thought-leadership with *The New Sustainability Advantage*,
an even more compelling updated case for businesses of all size to reap the
benefits of advancing sustainability. His thorough research and impeccable cre-
dentials have the power to both convince sceptics and arm champions. Bob's
well laid out balance of risk and opportunity inspires those businesses already
addressing sustainability issues to push further and deeper for even greater
triple-bottom-line impacts. By providing resources, worksheets
and on-line material to empower businesses to do it themselves,
Bob is proactively building the sustainable world he wants to live in.

—Barbara Turley McIntyre, Director Sustainability and Corporate Citizenship,
The Co-Operators Group Limited

Willard's latest update adds some important ideas to the field of
sustainability. He has assembled some of the best data and case studies
available on why and how sustainability creates enduring value for companies.
Before organizations can really commit and learn to compete on sustainability,
they need to really understand all aspects of the business case for driving
green deep into strategy. Willard's book is an indispensable resource
and an easy read, which doesn't go together often.

— Andrew Winston, environmental strategist and co-author of
the international bestseller *Green to Gold* .

Going green is highly profitable. Bob Willard documents this fact
in case study after case study: His analysis is spot on. Cutting carbon is
really a proxy for cutting energy and electricity — hence cutting cost.
With a good green story companies are raising revenue because consumers
want to buy from a company that isn't destroying the future of their children
and grandchildren. Going green also mitigates risk against rising energy
prices. So sustainability cut cost, raises revenue and mitigates risk.
This book is a must read for every executive who is concerned about
the bottom line — and their corporate license to operate.

— Jim Harris, International bestselling author,
Former Leader, Green Party of Canada

Praise for

The Sustainability Advantage (First Edition)

Bob Willard has performed a service of inestimable value: quantifying
the business case for sustainability. He shows how to capture the potential
effects of millions of firms, large and small, waking up to the untapped
profit potential that's all around them. Read this book to learn how.

—Ray Anderson, CEO, Interface, Inc.

Bob Willard has laid out a powerful but practical guide to the
ways in which companies can use the sustainability concept to improve
productivity and decrease expenses, while increasing revenue and shareholder
value. ... His book is a delightful combination of creativity and vigor.

—Stephan Schmidheiny, Honorary Chairman,
World Business Council for Sustainable Development

The Sustainability Advantage makies the most compelling argument
yet for how business can profit from a strategy that focuses on the health
of people and the planet. By putting these lessons into practice,
you'll save your company, you'll preserve the environment,
and you'll earn new respect for yourself.

—Jim Kouzes, co-author,
The Leadership Challenge and *Encouraging the Heart*

The *New* Sustainability Advantage

COMPLETELY REVISED 10TH ANNIVERSARY EDITION

The *New* Sustainability Advantage

SEVEN BUSINESS CASE BENEFITS OF A TRIPLE BOTTOM LINE

BOB WILLARD

new society
PUBLISHERS

Cover design by Diane McIntosh.
Main image: © iStock (Jim Schemel) rooster: © iStock (pastoor)

Printed in Canada. First printing February 2012.

New Society Publishers acknowledges the support of the Government of Canada through the Book Publishing Industry Development Program (BPIDP) for our publishing activities.

Paperback ISBN: 978-0-86571-712-1
eISBN: 978-1-55092-507-4

Inquiries regarding requests to reprint all or part of *The New Sustainability Advantage* should be addressed to New Society Publishers at the address below.

To order directly from the publishers, please call toll-free (North America) 1-800-567-6772, or order online at www.newsociety.com

Any other inquiries can be directed by mail to:
New Society Publishers
P.O. Box 189, Gabriola Island, BC V0R 1X0, Canada (250) 247-9737

Library and Archives Canada Cataloguing in Publication

Willard, Bob
    The new sustainability advantage : seven business case benefits of a triple bottom line / Bob Willard. – Completely rev. 10th anniversary ed.

Previous ed. published under the title: The sustainability advantage.
Includes bibliographical references and index.
ISBN 978-0-86571-712-1

    1. Management–Environmental aspects. 2. Sustainable development reporting.
3. Business enterprises–Environmental aspects. 4. Environmental protection–Economic aspects. 5. Sustainable development. I. Title.

HD30.255.W54 2012   658.4'083   C2011-908458-9

New Society Publishers' mission is to publish books that contribute in fundamental ways to building an ecologically sustainable and just society, and to do so with the least possible impact on the environment, in a manner that models this vision. We are committed to doing this not just through education, but through action. The interior pages of our bound books are printed on Forest Stewardship Council®-registered acid-free paper that is **100% post-consumer recycled** (100% old growth forest-free), processed chlorine free, and printed with vegetable-based, low-VOC inks, with covers produced using FSC®-registered stock. New Society also works to reduce its carbon footprint, and purchases carbon offsets based on an annual audit to ensure a carbon neutral footprint. For further information, or to browse our full list of books and purchase securely, visit our website at: www.newsociety.com

MIX
Paper from
responsible sources
FSC
www.fsc.org   FSC® C016245

To my wife, Sherrill,

who ensures that our personal sustainability flourishes.

Contents

Acknowledgments

Hundreds of conversations, articles, journals, books, and conferences contributed to this book — some directly, but most indirectly.

In the last ten years I have given over 700 interactive talks on the business case for sustainability strategies to corporate, non-governmental, academic, and public sector audiences. The question-and-answer sessions and informal conversations at these events were wonderful learning labs. I learned about the need to articulate my points more succinctly; to provide snappy evidence to back up my claims; to reframe my arguments so that they are more relevant to those in the discussion; and to listen and learn from their experiences.

Other speakers at these events also enriched my thinking. So did the authors of the thousands of articles I have perused, brought to my attention by the dozen or so press clipping services to which I subscribe. The explosion of material on corporate social responsibility (CSR); sustainable development; sustainability; and environmental, social, and governance (ESG) strategies provides excellent grist for my authorial mill.

I also acknowledge valuable help from Caroline Nolan, principal at ThinkSustain® Consulting, and Timothy Nash, president of Strategic Sustainable Investments. Not only did they provide me with data, material, and examples, but they were also invaluable sounding boards as I grappled with decisions about the flow, organization, emphasis, and quantification of the sustainability benefits. Tom Ewart, Tima Bansal, and Bushra Tobah at the Network for Business Sustainability helped clarify my understanding of academic research on the business value of sustainability programs and helped me separate relevant findings from the interesting but not-so-useful majority.

As usual, working with Heather Nicholas and her colleagues at New Society Publishers was a treat. It is fun to collaborate with kindred spirits. Diane McIntosh's artistic touches on the cover, and Audrey McClellan's eagle eye on the text provided professional polish to the finished product. They helped with all four of my books and are my trusted safety net.

Thank you all.

Preface to the Second Edition

When I did research for the first edition of *The Sustainability Advantage*, I relied on studies, cases, reports, and literature written in the late 1990s and early 2000s. Since then, sustainability strategies have become even more relevant to corporate success. New, compelling evidence of the potential business benefits convinced me to recalibrate the business case to reflect current findings.

My original plan was to update some of the examples in the original book and some of the parameters in the original spreadsheets. The evolution of the scope of the updates reminds me of what happened when my wife and I decided to make a few improvements to our home. We started by agreeing we should update the kitchen cupboards, but the more modern cupboards highlighted the age of the countertops, so we decided to replace them as well. Soon the kitchen flooring, appliances, and plumbing and lighting fixtures were on the list. Then it occurred to us that if we were going to redo the kitchen, we might as well remove the wall to the dining room and refinish the adjoining living room and its access to the back deck. An open, modernized downstairs layout would show up the dated hall entrance and staircase, and then we were talking about remodeling the upstairs. Whoa. That is when we realized that what we really wanted was a new house. So we moved.

Similarly, I quickly saw that it was easier to write a new manuscript than to update the previous one. This book is my new home for the business case for sustainability described in the first edition. The first edition was about why companies should embrace sustainability strategies. This edition focuses on why they are doing so and what additional benefits they might reap by going even further on their sustainability journeys. Figure 0.1 itemizes six ways that the new edition differs from the first.

One of my objectives in writing a 10th anniversary edition is to avoid the need for a 20th anniversary edition. The last point on the "what's new" list in Figure 0.1 references an online Sustainability Advantage Simulator dashboard and worksheets. They summarize the business case calculations described in *The New Sustainability Advantage* — think of the book as a detailed explanation of the simulator — and are freely available on my website at sustainabilityadvantage. com. If the logic and assumptions in the simulator need to be tuned to reflect new evidence, I can make adjustments immediately online. It is like a real-time précis of the book and an ongoing 10th anniversary edition.

FIGURE 0.1

What's New in the 10th Anniversary Edition

- *Updated:* It includes extensive updated examples and findings from reports, studies, surveys, articles, and other literature published in the last ten years.
- *New seven benefits:* It is organized around a new set of seven bottom-line benefits that align with current evidence about the most significant sustainability-related contributors to profit. It more thoroughly estimates the downside risk of not embracing the sustainability imperative, as well as six benefits of doing so.
- *Large companies and SMEs:* It calculates the potential bottom-line benefits for both large corporations and small- and medium-sized enterprises, where the first edition focused only on large companies.
- *Recalibrated worksheets, plus web-enabled dashboard:* Its companion Sustainability Advantage Simulator Worksheets are recalibrated, streamlined, and more user friendly than the previous worksheets. They are open-source and downloadable from sustainabilityadvantage.com. A new, abbreviated, web-enabled, interactive, slider-based Dashboard version of the Worksheets is also available on that website. Four composite examples of typical large and small companies in different industry sector groupings provide a choice of starting data profiles for the Worksheets and Dashboard.
- *Slides of graphics:* Its graphic figures are available in PowerPoint format for free from sustainabilityadvantage.com. Readers are encouraged to download and tailor them for their own purposes as sustainability champions. The slides are also included in Bob Willard's Master Slide Set, for use by its subscribers.
- *New two-page format:* It is reformatted in the same concise two-page, text-and-sidebar treatment of each subtopic that is used in *The Next Sustainability Wave* and *The Sustainability Champion's Guidebook.*

Preface

Picture this. It is five years from today. Your CEO was just interviewed by a writer from *Harvard Business Review* who is preparing an article for the next issue on the remarkable success of your business in an economy that wiped out some of your toughest competitors and ruthlessly downsized others.

You are a mid-level manager who helped orchestrate your company's turnaround. The writer is now interviewing you to get the straight goods on this magic "sustainable development" thing — is it really the silver bullet that other articles in the business press are claiming it is?

You describe the network of "Green Teams" in the company, which allow employees to work on facets of the company's overarching sustainability vision that particularly interest and energize them. Some teams focus on waste reduction, some on energy conservation, others on community programs. Collectively, they have implemented smart environmental and social initiatives, scaled up successful pilots, and convinced the CEO to champion further integration of sustainability strategies through the business and the company culture. You are happy that the CEO proudly took the lead in the company's transformation. If he had not, it would have taken a lot longer to achieve the impressive results.

The interview is fun — once you get the writer past the usual business press desire to find the one secret to the firm's success and the one leader-hero who made it happen. It is never that simple. At first it sounds like false modesty when you explain that it was a collaborative effort by everyone in the company and that many little things were instrumental to profit growth. When the writer asks for details and examples, though, the stories come alive (see Figure 0.2). There is so much to tell and so little time.

After the writer leaves, congratulating you on your recent appointment to Vice President Business Strategies, you realize that you forgot to mention how helpful it was to have a business case template that you initially used with the CEO and his C-suite colleagues to help them see how compelling the potential business benefits of sustainable development strategies were for their company. Oh well. You will make sure to start the interview with that story when you meet with the *Wall Street Journal* reporter who is coming tomorrow.

FIGURE 0.2

The Interview

You start by explaining how, five years ago, you and the CEO invited all employees to help revitalize the company's vision so that it inspired every manager and employee to pursue sustainable business goals.

You explain the company's commitment to a five-year investment in company-wide education on what sustainability means to society, to the business community, and especially to the firm and its stakeholders. Senior executives led discussions with employees on what the company was already doing on the "triple bottom line" (an expression that you needed to explain to the writer), what it planned to improve next, and how the company needed everyone's creative ideas and engagement to make it all happen. Progress reports by executives at the annual education sessions reinforced that this was not just another management fad and that empowering company-wide "Green Teams" was paying off. These training sessions were wonderful opportunities to celebrate progress on the sustainability journey.

You admit that you suspected some employees would be energized by the sustainability theme, but you were astonished by how it had raised the overall productivity of the company through individual and team efforts. People were voluntarily working harder and smarter to ensure the company did well and could continue to support environmental and social issues that they cared about. The opportunity to contribute to a better quality of life for their children and grandchildren unleashed their potential beyond any degree you had dreamed possible.

Over the last five years, revenue grew, expenses fell, and profits skyrocketed. Customer satisfaction reached new highs; the service and consulting arms of the business were now generating over half the revenue; and the volume of products that were leased surpassed the volume of outright sales. New products designed to appeal to "green customers" were helping to enhance the firm's brand image in the market and were, surprisingly, more profitable than most traditional products.

You show the reporter the numbers to back up these claims. She is impressed. Not only is this a feel-good story, it is a story about what kick-ass capitalism in pursuit of the common good can achieve. She'll have fun with this one.

Introduction

Business and industry — not just American business and industry,
but global business and industry — must change its ways to survive ...
And by survive I do not mean maintain identity and integrity within
the context of a financial system in meltdown, either.
By survive, I mean business must be steered through a transition
from an old and dangerously dysfunctional model to a far better
one that will operate in harmony with nature — thrive in a carbon-
constrained world, and put down the threats of global climate
disruption, species extinction, resource depletion, and
environmental degradation. In a word, develop a business
model that is sustainable.

— Ray Anderson, *Confessions of a Radical Industrialist*

Sustainability Strategies Are Smart Business Strategies

Sustainability strategies give companies a sustainable competitive advantage. The business benefits are quantifiable and real — the return on investment from aggressively improving company-wide sustainable development knowledge and initiatives makes other traditional investment opportunities seem trivial. Whichever company captures these benefits soonest has a significant competitive edge. Companies that ignore this reality are squandering easily achieved bottom-line benefits. Sustainability is a race to the top.

Businesspeople do not have to be transformed into tree-hugging environmental activists to reap these benefits. They can remain just what their shareholders expect them to be — hard-nosed executives who evaluate proposals on their bottom-line merits. Saving the world and making a profit is not an either/or proposition. It is a both/and proposition. Good environmental and social programs make good business sense. Benefits from more aggressive and creative attention to environmental and social projects create a win/win/win approach for the corporation, society, and the planet.

Addressing environmental and sustainability issues in a systematic way provides new opportunities to focus on core business objectives such as reducing hiring and retention costs, improving productivity, reducing expenses at manufacturing and commercial sites, increasing revenue and market share, reducing risk, and increasing profit. That is why CEOs want to fully embed sustainability into their company's strategies and operations, as shown in Figure 1.1. It is smart business.

One way to portray the evolution of company attention to sustainability is shown in Figure 1.2. Companies begin improving their legitimacy and image simply by ensuring they and their suppliers comply with human rights, environmental, and health and safety regulations in all their operations. Then they capitalize on eco-efficiencies to save money on their energy, water, materials, and waste bills. The exciting part is in the upper two quadrants. Companies practice disruptive innovation, reinvent their products and processes to improve their green attributes, and then take them to current and new underserved markets in the top right-hand quadrant.

In this chapter we expand these four quadrants into a more granular five-stage journey. First, we set the table for the buffet of sustainability benefits by clarifying terminology, frameworks, and our premise.

FIGURE 1.1

Significant CEO Mindset Shift

CEOs Agree /Strongly Agree that sustainability should be ....

■ 2010 ☐ 2007

2010 Increase Over 2007

... **fully embedded into company strategy and operations**

96%
72%

24%

... discussed and acted on by **boards**

93%
69%

24%

... fully embedded into **subsidiaries'** strategies and operations

91%
65%

26%

... embedded throughout the **global supply chain**

88%
59%

29%

... the basis for **industry collaborations** and **multi-stakeholder partnerships**

78%
56%

22%

... incorporated into discussions with **financial analysts**

72%
51%

21%

Source: Adapted from UN Global Compact–Accenture, "A New Era of Sustainability," June 2010, p. 32. Based on findings from a survey of 766 CEOs worldwide, including 50 in-depth interviews.

FIGURE 1.2

Four Quadrants of Enterprise Sustainability

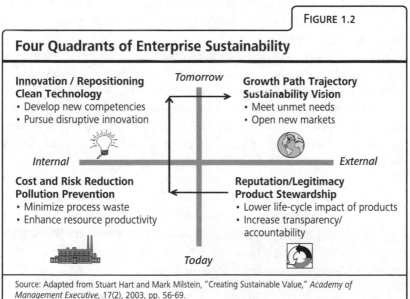

Innovation / Repositioning Clean Technology
• Develop new competencies
• Pursue disruptive innovation

Tomorrow

Growth Path Trajectory Sustainability Vision
• Meet unmet needs
• Open new markets

Internal — *External*

Cost and Risk Reduction Pollution Prevention
• Minimize process waste
• Enhance resource productivity

Reputation/Legitimacy Product Stewardship
• Lower life-cycle impact of products
• Increase transparency/ accountability

Today

Source: Adapted from Stuart Hart and Mark Milstein, "Creating Sustainable Value," *Academy of Management Executive*, 17(2), 2003, pp. 56-69.

The Premise

Our current economic model is unsustainable and is threatening our continued existence as a species. Governments have good intentions but are unable to lead — they are stripped of the needed tax revenues and are too beholden to status quo interests to be effective. Civil society has passion and good intentions but is up against huge vested forces that dominate communications channels. The only human enterprises that are large and powerful enough to effect the paradigm shift are enlightened businesses. More and more, business leaders influence world decisions. Without their support, restoring natural systems and healing social inequities takes longer and may be impossible. Time is running out. We need socially and environmentally responsible companies to be Trojan horses within the business community, leading the transformation to sustainability.

Because companies are "for profit," they are required to ensure their bottom lines are healthy enough to allow them to continue operating. Executives who lose track of that reality in the game of business soon find themselves watching the game from the sidelines. We need to equip enlightened executives with compelling numbers that show that sustainability-related strategies are smart business — that the company can do better by doing good; that a more responsible form of capitalism generates higher profits. They know that superior environmental and social performance leads to more goodwill with the company's important stakeholders listed in Figure 1.3. They also know that sustainability strategies improve revenue, reduce costs, and help them win the talent war, as highlighted in Figure 1.4.

To be convincing, we need to ensure we are talking the language of senior executives. We must quantify the benefits of a revolutionary transformation to a more sustainable and profitable business model in the new economy. We need to meet the executives where they are, use familiar frameworks to show the relevance of sustainability-related strategies to today's priorities, and show how the company can position itself to capitalize on going further on its sustainability journey.

Laggard companies are missing a business opportunity. If their shareholders woke up to what was being left on the table by company executives who marginalize sustainability-related strategies, they would not be pleased. The time has come to dispel the notion that being green is bad for business. If saving the planet is not reason enough, there's another incentive for companies to contribute to sustainable development — it boosts profits.

FIGURE 1.3

Stakeholders Driving Sustainability

Stakeholders who CEOs believe will have the greatest impact on the way they manage societal expectations

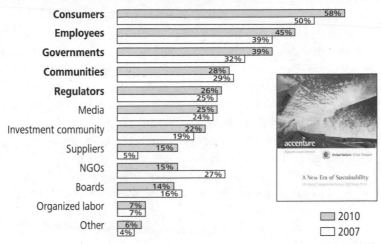

Stakeholder	2010	2007
Consumers	58%	50%
Employees	45%	39%
Governments	39%	32%
Communities	28%	29%
Regulators	26%	25%
Media	25%	24%
Investment community	22%	19%
Suppliers	15%	5%
NGOs	15%	27%
Boards	14%	16%
Organized labor	7%	7%
Other	6%	4%

☐ 2010
☐ 2007

Source: Adapted from UN Global Compact–Accenture, "A New Era of Sustainability," June 2010, p. 23. Based on findings from a survey of 766 CEOs worldwide, including 50 in-depth interviews.

FIGURE 1.4

Sustainability Drivers for CEOs

Top drivers of CEOs' action on sustainability issues

Driver	Percent
Brand, trust, and reputation	72%
Potential for revenue/growth/cost reduction	44%
Personal motivation	42%
Consumer/customer demand	39%
Employee engagement and recruitment	31%
Impact of development gaps	29%
Regulatory environment	24%
Pressure from investors	12%

Source: Adapted from UN Global Compact–Accenture, "A New Era of Sustainability," June 2010, p. 20. Based on findings from a survey of 766 CEOs worldwide, including 50 in-depth interviews.

Definitions, Terminology, and Frameworks

As sustainability champions, we are sometimes confronted by frustrated business people who ask what we mean by "sustainability." What they really want to know about is sustainability's relevance to them and their organization. Is it a threatening concept or a friendly one? Is it just a fancy, multiple-syllable word for something to which they are already paying attention?

As we attempt to clarify others' perceptions and misconceptions, it is helpful to have a few definitions in our vocabulary to facilitate the discussion. Figure 1.5 shows the meaning of "sustainable development" provided by the 1987 Report of the Brundtland Commission, *Our Common Future,* as well as two more definitions which supplement that touchstone. The word "flourish" in John Ehrenfeld's definition is uplifting and energizing. Chuck Hopkins' four-word definition is wonderfully memorable and succinct. A Google search will find hundreds of other good definitions.

The foundation of sustainability is implied by the definitions: all human activity needs to stay within the ecological carrying capacity of the planet, and it must not consume natural resources in excess of the ability of ecosystems to regenerate them. Anything else compromises both the ability of the present generation to meet its needs and the ability of future generations to meet theirs. We have already exceeded the carrying capacity of the planet by 50% and counting.[1] It is time to clean up our act.

The Natural Step, an international non-governmental organization, espouses four scientifically based system conditions that echo the fundamental components of sustainable development.[2]

- Nature's functions and diversity must not be subject to increasing concentrations of substances extracted from the earth's crust.
- Nature's functions and diversity must not be subject to increasing concentrations of substances produced by society.
- Nature's functions and diversity must not be impoverished by overharvesting or other forms of ecosystem manipulation.
- Resources must be used fairly and efficiently in order to meet basic human needs worldwide.

We are part of the whole, not separate from it. We cannot exist sustainably without the ecosystem services provided to us free of charge by clean air, clean water, clean soil, and fully functioning habitats. Preservation of those (even at current levels, as degraded as they are, based on what we know existed from historic record) is the big challenge that sustainable development attempts to address.

FIGURE 1.5

Definitions of Sustainability

Sustainable Development (SD)

Meeting the needs of the present generation without compromising the ability of future generations to meet their own needs.

Source: Gro Harlem Brundtland, *Our Common Future*, Report of the UN World Commission on Environment and Development, Oxford University Press,1987, p. 54.

Sustainability

The possibility that humans and other life will flourish on Earth forever.

Source: John Ehrenfeld, *Sustainability by Design*, Yale University Press, 2008, p. 49.

Sustainable Development (SD)

Enough, for all, forever.

Source: Charles Hopkins, "Enough, for All, Forever," *Education Canada*, 49(4), 2010, p. 42.

Definitions of a Sustainable Society

For years I have used the three-legged stool metaphor, shown in Figure 1.6, to illustrate the three dimensions of sustainability: economic, environmental, and social. (The three descriptors at the bottom of the figure are thought-provoking alternative labels for the stool.) The three-legged stool metaphor reinforces that society is unstable if one leg is weak. The downside of the metaphor is that it makes the economic, environmental, and social legs appear separate and equal.

Some sustainability champions use a Venn diagram of three overlapping circles to show sustainability, with circles representing the intersection of economic, environmental, and social factors. Depending on our mindset, we may resize the circles to show that one factor is more dominant than the other two. Unfortunately, a Venn diagram model implies that economic considerations should be "traded off" or "balanced" against environmental and social impacts, rather than "integrating" these three dimensions. The model also implies that the economy, society, and environment exist independently.

The three-nested-dependencies model in Figure 1.7 reflects a more interdependent reality. It depicts human society as a wholly owned subsidiary of the environment — without food, clean water, fresh air, fertile soil, and other natural resources, we are out of business. People in societies decide how they will exchange goods and services. That is, they create their economic models and change them if they find they are not working to improve their quality of life. To add another metaphor: society is the dog and the economy is the tail, not vice versa.

To be fair, the society–economy relationship is symbiotic. During the recent recession, the economic downturn had a significant impact on many people's quality of life. Good jobs are so important to a vibrant modern-day society that sustainability champions who portray the economy as subservient to society are sometimes accused of being naïve about how the "real world" works. It might be useful to remind critics of the famous picture of the Earth taken from space. That is our real "real world." The defining photo of our little blue home suspended in the universe shows just water, clouds, and land — the environment. People and the economy are invisibly nested within it.

The photo also reminds us of a stark reality: there is no umbilical cord going somewhere else, so we must live within the carrying capacity of the planet. Our continued existence depends on how well we steward our natural resources to ensure our social and economic sustainability. If we mess up, we are history. Not good.

FIGURE 1.6

Three-Legged Sustainability Stool

Sustainability

Environmental Leg
No pollution and waste
Enough energy and water
Conservation
Restoration

Economic Leg
Good jobs
Fair wages
Infrastructure
Fair trade

Social Leg
Working conditions
Health care
Education services
Community and culture
Social justice

Quality of Life/Genuine Wealth/Genuine Progress

FIGURE 1.7

Three-Nested-Dependencies Model

Environment

Human Society

Human Economy

Source: Adapted from Peter Senge, Bryan Smith, et al., *The Necessary Revolution*, Doubleday, 2008, p. 102.

Snorkeling in the Terminology Swamp

The three-legged stool metaphor applies to enterprises as well as to societies. In that context its legs are economic prosperity, environmental stewardship, and social responsibility, or Profit, Planet, and People, as illustrated in Figure 1.8.

The Profit element of the 3Ps is easily understood and accepted by companies — it is about the long-term financial health of the enterprise. The Planet dimension reminds companies to not only "do no harm" to the environment with their operations and products, but also to help restore the environment from harm already done. This requires reducing the amount of energy, water, and materials consumed in the manufacture of products, plus reducing waste and remediating contaminated sites. The People element encompasses how the company treats its employees, the working conditions and labor relations in its own operations and those of its suppliers, adherence to business ethics, and investment in communities it touches. The term "corporate social responsibility" (CSR) is rooted in this leg of the stool. However, in the last ten years CSR has become another umbrella term that recognizes the synergy of all three legs. Accordingly, it is often abbreviated to "corporate responsibility" (CR), embracing the social, environmental, and financial legs of the stool.

In business journals like *The Economist,* environmental, social, and governance (ESG) is the preferred label for the three-legged stool. Do ESG, CSR, CR, sustainable development (SD), and "green" all mean the same thing? Not quite, but they are close enough to capture the common essence of sustainability.

When we deal with hard-nosed business leaders, it behooves us to translate sustainability-speak into their business language of assets and capital, as shown in Figure 1.9. The use of business terminology helps companies recognize their direct or indirect dependence on natural capital for their energy, materials, food, and water. The term "natural capital" reinforces the wisdom of living off the Earth's interest, not its capital. Human capital is the company's engaged workforce. Social capital is the good reputation the firm has with its important stakeholders, like customers, communities, regulators, suppliers, and investors. By equating sustainability with asset management, we help connect the dots between smart business strategies (which foster the growth of all five capitals in Figure 1.9) and smart sustainability strategies (which do the same).

In this book, "sustainability" is our preferred umbrella term for the three dimensions of responsible companies. We occasionally use one of the other terms, just for variety.

FIGURE 1.8

Corporate Sustainability Three-Legged Stool

Sustainability = Sustainable Development (SD)
= Environmental, Social, Governance (ESG)
= Corporate Social Responsibility (CSR)
= Corporate Responsibility (CR) = Green
= Triple Bottom Line (TBL) = 3Es = 3Ps

Economy/Profits
Growth
Jobs
Taxes
Products
Services

Environment/Planet
Eco-efficiencies
Eco-effectiveness

Equity/People
Employees
Community
World

FIGURE 1.9

Smart Business Three-Legged Stool

Asset Management

Economic/Financial
capital
Built/Manufactured
capital

Natural capital

Human capital
Social capital

Sustainable Value Creation

Our Unsustainable Take-Make-Waste Business Model

The game of business as we have played it for the last 150 years cannot continue. It has been fun, but if we keep playing the exponential growth game, everyone loses. Overconsumption and poor resource management have resulted in unsustainable use of natural and social capital. Climate change puts further pressure on natural systems, upon which all our social systems and economies depend. We have limited time to avoid a global tipping point that could impact all of humankind, including future generations, adversely and permanently.

As Figure 1.10 shows, today's business model encourages companies to relentlessly deplete the natural capital that companies and communities require for their food, water, energy, and materials. Companies contribute directly or indirectly to systematic over-extraction and degradation of nature by physical means, such as deforestation, overharvesting of fish stocks, and depletion of farmlands. Nature is resilient and self-regenerative, but there is an ecological tipping point beyond which it cannot recover from this abuse. We are eating, and fouling, our own nest.

Excessive waste accumulates from things we dig up. Extractive businesses like mining and oil-and-gas companies notoriously leave tailings and other waste behind. Refineries, smelters, and manufacturing plants create more air, water, and soil pollution. When we burn natural resources for fuel, more waste is produced. Further, Earth's air, water, and soil are treated as dump sites by companies and their customers. Nature cannot absorb our pollutants fast enough to avoid their buildup. We must do a better job of managing those waste thresholds or we risk drowning in our own garbage. To quote David Brower, "There is no business to be done on a dead planet."[3]

Finally, the current business model interferes with peoples' needs being met. Many business models today contribute — directly or indirectly — to abuses of political or economic power that mean people don't have access to the clean air, potable water, nutritious food, adequate shelter, and quality of life they need. Today's business model encourages overconsumption by the haves at the expense of the have-nots. It is unsustainable.

To recap, today's take-make-waste business model is no longer feasible. It violates all four of The Natural Step's system conditions for a sustainable society. That contention is probably not the best conversation-opener with a senior business leader. But at some point along the line, sustainability champions should be ready to gently help executives break the hold of the unsustainable mental model of doing business.

FIGURE 1.10

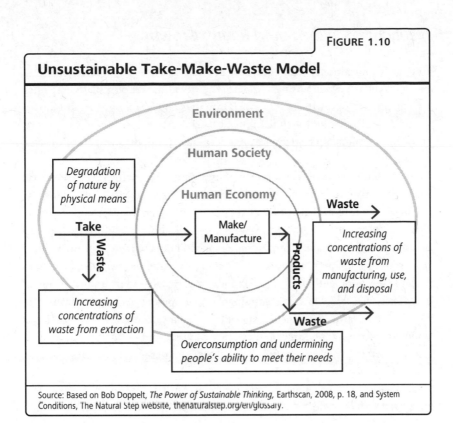

Unsustainable Take-Make-Waste Model

Environment

Human Society

Human Economy

Degradation of nature by physical means

Take

Waste

Make/ Manufacture

Products

Waste

Increasing concentrations of waste from manufacturing, use, and disposal

Increasing concentrations of waste from extraction

Overconsumption and undermining people's ability to meet their needs

Waste

Source: Based on Bob Doppelt, *The Power of Sustainable Thinking*, Earthscan, 2008, p. 18, and System Conditions, The Natural Step website, thenaturalstep.org/en/glossary.

Elephant #1 in the Board Room: Growth

In today's conventional business model, growth is a given, an imperative. "Grow or die" is the maxim of business leaders. The stock market punishes companies that do not meet growth expectations. Growth is good. Since growth is synonymous with progress and with winning in today's game of business, we need to show how sustainability strategies are relevant and support companies' growth goals.

Continuous growth is at odds with sustainability principles. We know that it is inherently unsustainable, given the finite carrying capacity of the planet. In medicine, continuous growth is called cancer, but this analogy is the elephant in many board rooms, something managers don't talk about. Passionate, principled champions of sustainability find it repugnant to help companies grow, because it is against their core values to do so. That is why some shy away from the "sustainable development" label — development implies growth, and continuous growth is unsustainable. Ergo, "sustainable development" is an oxymoron.

Not necessarily. Sustainable enterprises decouple revenue growth from depletion of natural resources and creation of waste and pollution. Their products and services improve the quality of life for their employees, customers, and the communities they serve. They grow while decreasing their ecological and social footprints. Their rate of material throughput — the metabolism of the industrial system — does not endanger society, prosperity, and quality of life.

As I will show in this book, sustainable companies can nudge unsustainable competitors off the playing field because they spend less on resources and grow their revenue faster. That is a good thing. However, at some point even the continuous growth of more sustainable companies will be problematic. The planet cannot sustain the growing demand for its non-renewable natural capital nor can it continue to absorb more and more waste. Unless companies are resource, energy, and water neutral, and produce zero waste and zero pollution, we overshoot the carrying capacity of the planet.

Prosperity without Growth? was the title of a 2010 report from the Sustainable Development Commission that offers creative alternatives to continuous growth.[4] As outlined in Figure 1.11, Peter Victor's book *Managing Without Growth* shows how the growth imperative has failed us. Richard Heinberg's book *The End of Growth* goes further and shows why continuous growth is blocked by resource depletion, environmental impacts, and rising levels of debt.[5] That leads us to the second undiscussable elephant in the room: overconsumption.

FIGURE 1.11

Continuous Growth Does Not Work

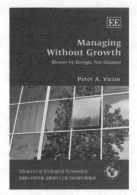

Rich countries should turn away from economic growth as the primary policy objective and **pursue more specific objectives that enhance well-being:**

1. Continued economic growth worldwide is unrealistic due to environmental and resource constraints.

2. Rising incomes increase happiness and well-being only up to a level that has since been surpassed in rich countries.

3. Economic growth has not brought full employment, eliminated poverty, or reduced the burden of the economy on the environment.

Source: Based on Peter A. Victor, *Managing Without Growth,* Edward Elgar, 2008, pp. 154–155.

Elephant #2 in the Board Room: Overconsumption

Consumption is the root cause of growth, since companies grow when the demand for their products grows. However, overconsumption is the second elephant that no one in the board room is talking about. A UN report warns that by 2050, humans could triple the amount of natural resources they consume unless economic growth is decoupled from resource use and current consumption rates.[6] Warning that global population growth and rising economic prosperity could drive resource consumption far beyond what is sustainable on a finite Earth, the report states that nations must improve their rate of resource productivity — in other words, do more with less.

Excuses for rapacious consumption come in many guises. President Eisenhower encouraged consumerism as a way to address the 1950s recession. President Bush encouraged it after 9/11 as a patriotic duty to fight another economic speed bump. Increased consumption has become politicians' panacea for economic slowdowns. If there is no consumer demand for a company's goods and services, it stops producing them and lays off its workers. Laid-off workers cannot afford to buy goods and services, exacerbating the downward economic spiral.

We also justify consumption as a fun time-filler; a quest for social status; artificial fulfillment of psychological needs; a means of keeping up with the Joneses; or a way to reward ourselves for minor accomplishments. Whatever the reason, a want-borrow-buy mentality has given many consumers a severe case of "affluenza." They are borrowing themselves into perilous debt. Our neverending spending spree precipitates social and economic ruin.

When consumption takes on a life of its own, we risk overshooting the carrying capacity of the planet, as Mathis Wackernagel and William Rees argue in *Our Ecological Footprint*, illustrated in Figure 1.12. In part, this is because we do not really "consume" most goods. Rather, we use them and throw them away. The resulting buildup of waste is not sustainable. Annie Leonard's *The Story of Stuff* video illustrates how overconsumption contributes to social and environmental degradation.[7]

It is time we matured out of our unsustainable "gimme" culture. We need to shift our overconsumption mindset, portrayed by Ehrlich's IPAT formula, to Ray Anderson's version, as shown in Figure 1.13. We need a business paradigm that thrives on this more fulfilling need-save-buy approach to consumption of basic goods and services. Read on.

FIGURE 1.12

Overconsumption Leads to Overshoot

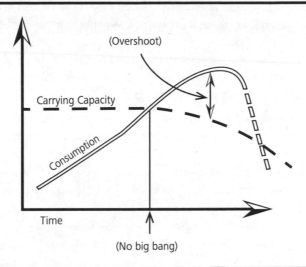

(Overshoot)

Carrying Capacity

Consumption

Time

(No big bang)

Source: Adapted from Mathis Wackernagel and William Rees, *Our Ecological Footprint,* New Society Publishers, 1996, p.54.

FIGURE 1.13

A Happier IPAT Formula

Ehrlich's original formula:

$$I = P \times A \times T$$

Source: Paul Ehrlich and John Holdren, "Impact of Population Growth" in *Population, Resources, and the Environment,* US Government Printing Office, 1972, pp. 365–377.

Ray Anderson's "more happiness, less stuff" version:

$$I = (P \times a \times T_1) \div T_2$$

I: Impact on the environment
P: Population
A: Affluence driven by wants
a: Responsible affluence driven by needs
T and T1: Technology/stuff
T2: Sustainable, renewable, recyclable technology

Source: Ray Anderson, "More Happiness, Less Stuff"[accessed July 30, 2011], EnvironmentalLeader.com.

A Sustainable Borrow-Use-Return Business Model

It is one thing to criticize the dominant take-make-waste business model as unsustainable; it is another thing to design a model that is sustainable. As sustainability champions, we need to have a positive vision of the pot of gold at the end of a sustainability rainbow — a vision that does not depend on continuous growth and overconsumption. Here are five characteristics of a sustainable, cyclical, borrow-use-return business model that is better for the environment, society, and the company (illustrated in Figure 1.14).

1. **Radical resource productivity.** Companies stretch natural resources by increasing productivity for a given amount of a resource by factors of 4, 10, or even 100.

2. **Investment in natural capital.** Companies protect and restore ecosystems to sustain societal and business needs. They decouple economic growth from depletion of the global commons.

3. **Ecological redesign.** Companies eliminate human-made toxic chemicals from their production processes, minimize use of resources and energy, use closed-loop production systems, and decrease waste and harmful emissions.

4. **Service and flow economy.** When products become obsolete or unable to perform their intended service, the company takes them back and recycles or remanufactures the returned products.

5. **Responsible consumption.** Although it sounds like an oxymoron, responsible consumption reduces the demand for stuff and its associated pollution. Consumers make better-informed decisions based on a product's place of origin, the labor conditions under which it was made, its ingredients, its packaging, its life-cycle ecological footprint, and other sustainability-related criteria.

New forms of company ownership and profit-sharing ensure company success is more equitably distributed. Resilient, locally owned enterprises are more accountable and devoted to serving community needs. Ethics, fairness, and transparency are baked into day-to-day governance systems, partnerships, community relations, and employment practices. Employees are treated like valuable contributors to the company's success, and reward and recognition systems are aligned to encourage environmentally and socially responsible decisions and behaviors.

Such a model is a win-win-win for the environment, society, and the company. The company helps restore the economic, ecological, and social health of the planet. And it makes more profit. The business case for sustaining the planet is stronger than the business case for trashing it.

FIGURE 1.14

Sustainable Borrow-Use-Return Model

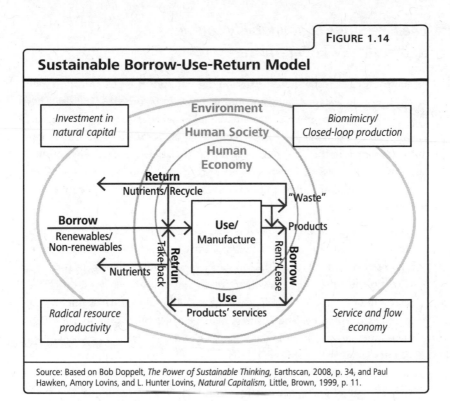

Source: Based on Bob Doppelt, *The Power of Sustainable Thinking*, Earthscan, 2008, p. 34, and Paul Hawken, Amory Lovins, and L. Hunter Lovins, *Natural Capitalism*, Little, Brown, 1999, p. 11.

The Five-Stage Sustainability Journey to a Sustainable Enterprise

As companies progress to become sustainable enterprises, we can position them on the five-stage sustainability continuum shown in Figure 1.15. Their business framework evolves from an unsustainable take-make-waste model in Stages 1, 2, and 3 to a sustainable borrow-use-return model in Stages 4 or 5. Executive mindsets, which in the early stages see initiatives labeled "green," "environmental," and "sustainable" as expensive and bureaucratic impediments to success, also evolve to recognize these initiatives as catalytic investments for competitive advantage.

- **Stage 1: Pre-Compliance.** The company cuts corners and tries not to get caught if it breaks the law or uses exploitative practices that cheat the system. It flouts environmental, health, and safety regulations. This stage is the norm in corrupt jurisdictions. Elsewhere, intelligent companies move quickly to Stage 2 in order to avoid fines, prosecution, and public embarrassment.
- **Stage 2: Compliance.** The business manages its liabilities by obeying labor, environmental, health, and safety regulations in the jurisdictions in which it operates. It has an environmental management system and company policies on environmental protection and human rights. It reactively does what it is legally bound to do while happily externalizing its ecological and social collateral damage. It installs pollution abatement equipment as end-of-pipe retrofits. Stage 2 is the baseline.
- **Stage 3: Beyond compliance.** A company voluntarily moves to Stage 3 when it realizes that it can save money with proactive operational eco-efficiencies, or at least avoid a public relations crisis and discourage new regulations. It reaps incremental "low-hanging fruit" by saving energy while reducing its associated carbon footprint; saving water; saving materials in its products and packaging; and saving waste costs.

Stage 3 companies focus efforts where they can generate big results, fast. In Stage 3, sustainability initiatives are usually marginalized within specialized departments. They are tacked on as green housekeeping, rather than being institutionalized in the company's governance systems.

Companies in Stage 3 are not sustainable; they are just less unsustainable. Many Stage 3 companies have annual targets for further waste and electricity reduction and for the further elimination of toxic substances used in manufacturing, but the goals are increasingly difficult to meet. The law of diminishing returns inhibits further savings from eco-efficiency programs. A new phase must be entered. That is why companies aspire to Stage 4.

FIGURE 1.15

Five-Stage Sustainability Journey

5. Purpose/Passion
Align with founder's/CEO's values

 4. Integrated Strategy
Enhance company value/prosperity

3. Beyond Compliance
Save with eco-efficiencies
Avoid PR crisis
Avoid threat of new regulations

2. Compliance
Avoid fines, prosecution, bad PR

1. Pre-Compliance

Source: Based on Bob Willard, *The Sustainability Champion's Guidebook,* New Society Publishers, 2009, p. 11.

Stages 4 and 5:
Similar Behaviors, Different Motivations

About 90% of the behaviors of Stage 4 and Stage 5 companies look the same. Companies in both stages adopt a cyclical, borrow-use-return model of sustainable capitalism. They inject sustainability principles into their cultural DNA. Companies in both stages deploy business strategies that respect the environment, the community, and the ongoing business health of the firm. They unleash the untapped creative energies of all employees and managers, empowering them to suggest and implement sustainability-oriented expense-saving and revenue-growing opportunities. Sustainability expectations are aligned within the organization and across the entire value chain. Instead of seeing green costs and risks, companies in both stages see investments and opportunities. They make cleaner, greener products, and they embrace eco-effectiveness and life-cycle stewardship. They are sustainable enterprises doing no harm, doing good, and making more profit.

It is the motivations of companies in these two stages that differ, as represented by the dotted line between Stage 4 and Stage 5 in Figure 1.16. The means and the ends — the benefits and the co-benefits — of companies in the two stages are flipped. Think of Stage 4 companies as publicly traded companies that are chartered to put their shareholders' interests first and ensure they reap competitive advantages from their sustainability initiatives. Think of Stage 5 companies as founder-owned companies with a priority on values-based corporate citizenship.

Many Stage 5 companies do not go through the first four stages. They start and end in Stage 5. Many of them are in the 98% to 99% of companies in the world that are small or medium-sized businesses. Some become famous (see Figure 1.17). Their company values mirror the values of their founders. If you were to congratulate CEOs of small Stage 5 companies for being sustainable enterprises, many would have no idea what you were talking about. They do not frame their strategies and behaviors in those terms. They just do it. Publicly traded companies may evolve to Stage 5 once the legitimacy of social and environmental purposes is embraced in the business community. Benefit Corporations (B Corps) embody this trend.[8]

Does it matter whether a company is in Stage 4 or Stage 5? We would all like companies to do the right things for the right reasons, but Earth does not care. Our priority is to quickly reach the tipping point of a critical mass of sustainable firms to ensure a sustainable planet. Whatever convinces Stage 3 companies to aspire to Stage 4 will do. At Stage 4, they can see the wisdom of transforming to Stage 5 later.

FIGURE 1.16

Ends/Motivations vs. Means/Behaviors

Stage 5. Purpose/Passion

End: Contribute to a better world

Means: Be a successful company

Stage 5 companies do the right things because they're the right things to do; they're also good for the company.

— — — — — — — — — — — — — — —

Stage 4. Integrated Strategy

End: Be a successful company

Means: Contribute to a better world

Stage 4 companies do the right things because they're good for the company; they're also the right things to do.

FIGURE 1.17

Examples of Stage 5 Companies

	Company	Founders
	Ben & Jerry's Ice Cream	Ben Cohen and Jerry Greenfield
	The Body Shop	Anita Roddick
	Interface	Ray Anderson
	Seventh Generation	Jeffrey Hollender
	Patagonia	Yvon Chouinard
	New Society Publishers	Chris and Judith Plant

The Four-Step Transformation from Stage 3 to Stage 4

Is it really possible for a for-profit company to become a sustainable enterprise — to make the radical leap from Stage 3 to Stage 4 on its sustainability journey? Yes, but it requires a significant transformation. Each of the four intermediate stepping-stones between Stage 3 and Stage 4 (shown in Figure 1.18) is designed to produce real business benefits.

- **Stage 3.0: Improve company eco-efficiencies and sustainability brand.** In this stage, the firm captures energy, water, materials, and waste handling eco-efficiencies within the company's current internal operations and processes. Carbon footprint reductions usually accompany energy reductions in anticipation of a government-imposed price on carbon emissions. The company produces the same products and services and uses the same processes, but it does these more efficiently, passing the savings straight to its bottom line.

- **Stage 3.1: Improve supply chain conditions and footprints.** Acknowledging responsibility for the environmental and social impacts of its products throughout their life cycles, the company implements sustainable procurement practices. It works with suppliers to help them achieve the same eco-efficiencies that the company itself realized in Step 3.0. Suppliers are encouraged — or coerced — to clean up their acts or else risk losing the firm as a business-to-business (B2B) customer.

- **Stage 3.2: Create new eco-effective products, services, and leases.** The company redesigns its products and reengineers its processes to be radically more eco-effective, rather than simply eco-efficient. It co-creates new green products and services by collaborating with diverse stakeholders. Innovation abounds. The company reinvents itself, providing useful products and services in existing markets and in new, strategic markets. It leases products instead of selling them, and takes them back at the end of their useful life.

- **Stage 3.3: Embed sustainable governance.** The firm bakes sustainability into its decision making, its policies, and its culture. The company embeds sustainability principles in its financial measurement and management systems. It aligns its recognition, reward, evaluation, and remuneration systems to ensure everyone understands that sustainability considerations are important. Executive teams and boards revamp the company's governance system to assess — and transparently report on — how the firm is contributing to a sustainable global economy, society, and the environment.

The four stepping-stones may be taken serially or in parallel. They may be looped, with more being accomplished on each step during each pass. The speed and sequence of the steps will vary. But they are all touched sooner or later.

FIGURE 1.18

Five-Stage Sustainability Journey

5. Purpose/Passion
Align with founder's/CEO's values

4. Integrated Strategy
Enhance company value/prosperity

3.3: Embed sustainable governance
3.2: Create new eco-effective products,
  services, and leases
3.1: Improve supply chain conditions
  and footprints
3.0: Improve company eco-efficiencies
  and sustainability brand

3. Beyond Compliance
Capture eco-efficiencies; avoid PR and
regulatory risks

2. Compliance

1. Pre-Compliance

The Need for a Relevant, Aligned Business Case

Though some companies recognize the opportunity and adopt some eco-efficiency initiatives in Stage 3.0, they do not fully exploit innovation, new market development, new services, and new technologies until Stage 3.2. One reason businesses do a slow-motion launch of sustainability strategies is that they lack an appropriate business case to quantify the benefit opportunities. Saving the world is a daunting agenda for any business, especially at a time when corporations are scrambling for market share in an increasingly competitive environment. Proposing a new direction that might put your company out of business in order to save the world is a career-ending strategy.

It does not help when occasional articles resurrect Friedman-esque anti-CSR proclamations that "the business of business is business." For example, in his 2010 *Wall Street Journal* article "The Case against Corporate Social Responsibility," Aneel Karnani declared: "The idea that companies have a responsibility to act in the public interest and will profit from doing so is fundamentally flawed."[9] Of course there was a flurry of rebuttals, rebuttals to the rebuttals, and so on. Usually the author finally admits that he was using terminology differently, or he was simply echoing the common misperception that doing good and doing well is an either-or proposition, or he was confusing means with ends. But by then the debate has resurrected the fear of deviating from the norm and has portrayed enlightened leaders as naïve and misguided do-gooders. What nonsense.

The business benefits of sustainability initiatives need to be identified; they also need to be quantified and expressed in business language as bottom-line benefits relevant to the short- and long-term priorities of senior executives. If a strategy does not help the business, it is not going to survive on business leaders' radar screens. The trick is to focus on "enlightened self-interest" and bottom-line benefits. Environmental and social co-benefits can be happy by-products; they don't need to be the initial motivating rationale.

Money and numbers are the language of business, but most environmentalists know less about accounting than accountants know about the environment. Figure 1.19 shows the kind of metrics that will help convince companies that sustainability is a business opportunity, not an issue to be managed.

This book shows how big those benefits can be. It presents quantifiable evidence that investing in sustainable development pays off with real bottom-line benefits for those companies with the courage and foresight to embrace sustainability-related strategies.

FIGURE 1.19

Energy Savings at IBM

In 2010, IBM had 2,100 energy conservation projects at 299 locations that delivered savings equal to 5.7% of the company's total energy use versus the corporate goal of 3.5%. These projects avoided more than 139,000 metric tons of CO_2 emissions and saved $29.7 million in energy expenses.

Between 1990 and 2010, IBM saved 5.4 billion kWh of electricity consumption, avoided nearly 3.6 million metric tons of CO_2 emissions (equal to 52% of the company's 1990 global CO_2 emissions), and saved $399 million through its annual energy conservation actions.

Source: "Energy and Climate Programs" [accessed July 30, 2011], IBM.com.

Aligned with Existing Business Priorities

To entice companies toward Stage 4, we need to show how sustainability-related strategies are relevant to, and help address, their current priorities. What are those priorities? Figure 1.20 shows business priorities in 2011 for a cross-section of 2,691 senior executives in Europe, North America, and Asia. At first glance, the list is disappointing to sustainability champions: improving sustainability is not a high priority for companies. In a list of the top 10 priorities for executives, it is in 10th place, trumped by revenue growth, customer retention, and cost cutting.

The phrase "Sell the sizzle, not the steak" is a common sales adage. When we buy a light bulb, we do not really want a light bulb; we want the light it provides. Similarly, when selling sustainability to for-profit companies, we need to position it as a set of strategies that enable existing goals, not as another goal to worry about. Corporate decision makers do not buy sustainability strategies to "improve corporate environmental sustainability and social responsibility"; they are attracted to them because they are levers to attain their other nine priorities sooner and better. They strive for Stage 4 on their sustainability journeys when their chartered corporate purpose is still to maximize shareholder value, but once they've achieved Stage 4, they realize it's only a stepping stone to Stage 5, where the company's purpose becomes maximizing *stake*holder value, and where sustainability is seen as a goal in its own right rather than a set of enabling strategies.

To reach Stage 4 we need to link sustainability-related improvements to other business goals with a higher priority. For example, we need to show how sustainability-related strategies improve a company's ability to acquire and retain talent (priority #7); lower the firm's overall operating costs (priority #3); and help the company acquire and retain customers (priority #2). This book explains how to make those arguments.

This is the magic of the sustainability sale — it is not about sustainability. Sustainability is simply the means to high-priority business ends, not an end unto itself. To make it easy for executives to see the relevance of sustainability-related strategies and their benefits, it helps to map those benefits as enablers within familiar frameworks. We look at two next:

- The standard value chain framework, linking prerequisites to business success
- The standard income statement framework, used to calculate bottom-line profit

Later, in the chapter on risk mitigation (Benefit 7), we discuss a third framework for a standard business case that is used to make any business decision.

FIGURE 1.20

Top 10 Business Priorities for 2011

Category	Top Two Priorities by Category	Percentage Selecting
Growth	Grow overall company revenue	64%
	Acquire and retain customers	54%
Efficiency	Lower the firm's overall operating costs	44%
	Improve quality of products and/or processes	37%
Innovation	Improve our ability to innovate as an organization	32%
	Drive new market offerings or business practices	28%
Talent	Acquire and retain talent	38%
	Improve workforce productivity	31%
Transparency	Comply with governance regulations and requirements	14%
	Improve corporate environmental sustainability and social responsibility	**10%**

Source: Christopher Mines, "Sustainability Doesn't Sell ... or Does It?" [accessed July 30, 2011], GreenBiz.com. Based on Forrester's survey of 2,691 executives in Europe, North America, and Asia, in "Forrsights Business Decision-Makers Survey, Q4 2010."

Aligned with the Standard Value Chain Framework

Figure 1.21 shows a standard, generic business value chain. It is based on several other value chain frameworks and captures the most important elements from each. Its components are what it takes for any company to be successful. It is generic — it applies to any for-profit company, in any industry, anywhere. Do you want to start a company? Do you want it to be successful? Be good at each link in the value chain and you will succeed.

Following the chain from left to right, the company takes guidance from the market and develops the vision, goals, values, strategies, and systems that enable its success. If it is a manufacturing company, it makes quality products from raw materials, energy, and water. Companies in every sector want to attract, retain, and engage talented employees to produce and deliver their goods and services and to support customers. An unfortunate by-product of the company's operations is waste. On the other hand, if the company's products and services delight customers, the resulting revenue stream leads to the goal on the right-hand side — bottom-line profits.

Executives are continuously looking for ways to make the company's value chain more robust and resilient. Smart sustainability strategies and programs can help strengthen key links in the chain. Each of the seven benefits associated with strategic sustainability programs can be arrayed beside the link in the value chain that it most promotes, as shown in Figure 1.22.

Aligning sustainability-related benefits with the value chain framework makes it evident how and where each benefit strengthens important links. Being able to relate the "so what?" of sustainability benefits to the standard value chain enhances their business importance. By showing how sustainability-related strategies lead to benefits that are helpful to key elements in their current business model, we gain executives' support and accelerate their adoption of sustainability-based approaches. We make sustainability relevant.

Figure 1.22 reinforces a fundamental insight: social and environmental initiatives are not something a typical company pays attention to out of the goodness of its heart — they are business imperatives if a firm wants a winning value chain in today's game of business. The benefit of sustainability initiatives is that they strengthen the links in the value chain. Their co-benefit is that they are also good for the environment and society.

FIGURE 1.21

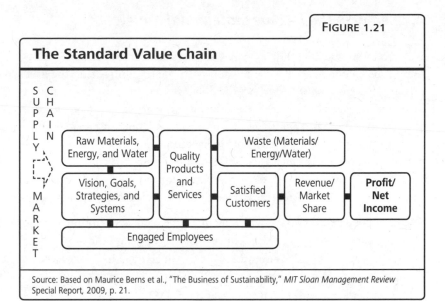

The Standard Value Chain

Source: Based on Maurice Berns et al., "The Business of Sustainability," *MIT Sloan Management Review Special Report*, 2009, p. 21.

FIGURE 1.22

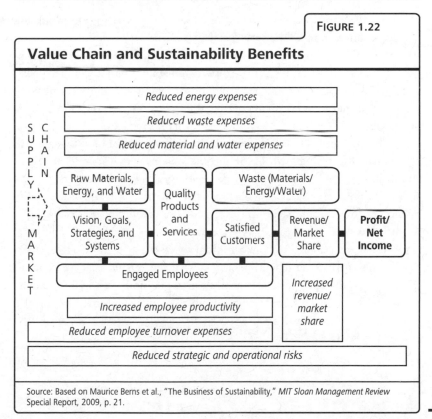

Value Chain and Sustainability Benefits

Source: Based on Maurice Berns et al., "The Business of Sustainability," *MIT Sloan Management Review Special Report*, 2009, p. 21.

Aligned with the Income Statement Framework

We need to make it easy for CEOs, CFOs, and other numbers-oriented executives in the C-suite to see how sustainability strategies contribute to the firm's success. That is, we need to connect the dots between a typical financial statement and the benefits that can be realized from smart environmental, social, and governance (ESG) approaches and programs. Aligning sustainability benefits with income statement elements helps executives see how sustainability initiatives are relevant to their current financial priorities.

Figure 1.23 shows the basic elements of an income statement, also known as a profit-and-loss (P&L) statement. Accountants use three categories of expenses.

- Cost of goods sold (COGS), which includes the costs of acquiring and producing the inventory of goods/products that the company sells
- Selling, general, and administrative (SG&A), which include the costs of running the company
- Interest, tax, depreciation, and amortization (ITDA)

A manufacturing company would realize the biggest savings from sustainability initiatives in its COGs expenses, which include the cost of labor, energy, water, and material to acquire and produce the goods it sells. A services company would see most of the savings from sustainability initiatives in its SG&A expenses, since COGS are much less significant for a non-manufacturing company. For our purposes, we do not need to differentiate between COGS, SG&A, and ITDA, so we combine them into one group of "Expenses."

Each of the seven benefits associated with smart sustainability strategies can be aligned with the element of the income statement that it most affects, as shown in Figure 1.24. The graphic makes evident how each benefit contributes to a more positive profit. Being able to relate the "so what?" of sustainability benefits to the income statement enhances the credibility of sustainability champions.

The income statement is the core framework that we use in the business case for sustainability. It determines the flow of the benefits that we examine. We start by looking at how sustainability strategies improve top-line revenue opportunities; then we monetize the benefits of reducing expenses and mitigating risks that might jeopardize profit.

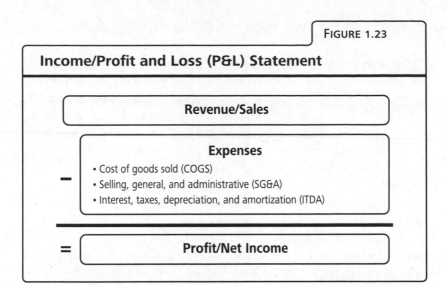

FIGURE 1.23

Income/Profit and Loss (P&L) Statement

Revenue/Sales

− **Expenses**
• Cost of goods sold (COGS)
• Selling, general, and administrative (SG&A)
• Interest, taxes, depreciation, and amortization (ITDA)

= **Profit/Net Income**

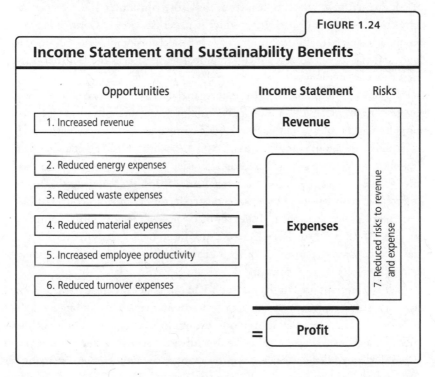

FIGURE 1.24

Income Statement and Sustainability Benefits

Opportunities	Income Statement	Risks
1. Increased revenue	**Revenue**	
2. Reduced energy expenses		
3. Reduced waste expenses		
4. Reduced material expenses	− **Expenses**	7. Reduced risks to revenue and expense
5. Increased employee productivity		
6. Reduced turnover expenses		
	= **Profit**	

Possibilities for Two Typical Companies

The business case is about *possibilities*, not probabilities. We look at the *potential* benefits of employing best practices already used by leading companies. Real companies are already achieving each of the claimed benefits. We are simply projecting the *potential* profit improvements if a typical company decides to use the complete suite of best sustainability practices. We look at the bottom-line benefits that a company could achieve within three to five years if it commits to becoming a sustainable enterprise. Happily, most benefits flow sooner. A five-year horizon is strategically long enough to allow new initiatives to gain the necessary traction to yield the described results, but soon enough that it is within most companies' attention span.

To illustrate the possibilities, we run the numbers for two composite companies at opposite ends of the company-size and materials-intensity spectrums. "Sam's Solutions" represents a small company in the professional services sector. It doesn't make products; it provides advisory, consulting, and professional services to other companies. Its product is expertise. "M&D Corp." is a large manufacturing, retail, distribution, or wholesale corporation. Its product is goods. Using these two very different companies reinforces the fact that business case methodology is scalable and industry independent.

Figures 1.25 and 1.26 show the basic financial data for our two generic companies. The Sustainability Advantage Simulator at sustainabilityadvantage.com provides data profiles of four sample generic companies as starter sets with which to initialize the online simulator dashboard and worksheets. The financial data for the sample companies is based on extensive analysis of profiles of companies in the TSX 60, S&P 500, Statistics Canada, and BizMiner databases for different-sized companies in various industry sectors. Numerous conversations with business people confirmed the reasonableness of the normalized company profiles. Of course, if you have data for a specific company, use it to override the data for the sample company in order to see the potential benefits from sustainability strategies for your company.

All assumptions used in the benefit calculations are conservative. Why? Our low-ball assumptions generate profit improvements that are astounding enough. If we used more probable assumptions, we might strain the credibility of the methodology. As well, we would like executives to receive a pleasant surprise when they override the simulator's starter set of data with their own company's data; replace the simulator's assumptions with their own experience, judgment, and gut instincts; and discover that the real business case is even more compelling than the simulator's.

FIGURE 1.25

Sam's Solutions Profile

Revenue	$1,000,000	Percentage of Revenue
Energy expense	$20,000	2%
Materials and water expense	$50,000	5%
Total salary / payroll expense	$300,000	30%
Profit	$70,000	7%
Average salary, including benefits	$50,000	
Number of employees	6	

FIGURE 1.26

M&D Corp. Profile

Revenue	$500,000,000	Percentage of Revenue
Energy expense	$10,000,000	2%
Materials and water expense	$150,000,000	30%
Total salary / payroll expense	$150,000,000	30%
Profit	$35,000,000	7%
Average salary, including benefits	$40,000	
Number of employees	3,750	

Increased Revenue and Market Share

*Think about sustainability as the common ground shared by your
business interests (those of your financial stakeholders) and the interests
of the public (your nonfinancial stakeholders). This common ground is
what we call the sustainability sweet spot: the place where the
pursuit of profit blends seamlessly with the pursuit of
the common good.*

— Andrew Savitz, *The Triple Bottom Line*

Revving-Up Revenue

A powerful rationale for sustainable development is enlightened self-interest, fed by the prospect of higher profits. Reducing expenses is one way to improve profits (and we quantify those possibilities in later chapters), but as the saying goes, you can't save your way to prosperity. That is why business strategy is often driven by bolstering revenue more than by cutting costs. Accordingly, and following the flow of the income statement in Figure 2.1, the first sustainability benefit we examine is increased revenue and market share.

In the Introduction we discussed how sustainable enterprises handle the tricky issues of growth and overconsumption. Sustainable enterprises disconnect revenue growth from depletion of natural resources by drastically reducing the amount of natural resources required to make their products and by using resource- and energy-efficient manufacturing processes. They decouple revenue growth from waste, pollution, and the depletion of natural capital by taking back their products at the end of their useful lives and ensuring they are responsibly disposed of, or reused.

Markets are fickle. Societal expectations change. Companies should anticipate those changes and develop new practices, new products, new markets, and new services in advance. Doing this before competitors do is the key to revenue growth and to sustained profits. However, when market leaders take action, their competitors often follow suit. The half-life of competitive differentiation is becoming shorter as reverse engineering and corporate intelligence improve. As soon as competitors have similar responsible practices and offerings, any competitive advantage is lost. Companies must continuously innovate to maintain their leadership position.

In this chapter we look at three innovative revenue streams that help ensure higher profits for sustainability leaders.

1. More business-to-consumer (B2C) and business-to-business (B2B) revenue from a more sustainable brand
2. New revenue from new green products
3. New revenue from services and leasing

FIGURE 2.1

Income Statement Framework

Revenue/Sales

−

Expenses
- Cost of goods sold (COGS)
- Selling, general, and administrative (SG&A)
- Interest, taxes, depreciation, and amortization (ITDA)

=

Profit/Net income

More B2C and B2B Revenue from a More Sustainable Brand

A sustainable brand makes a difference in the B2C sector. Increasingly, people prefer to do business with companies that are doing good things and are responsible. The responsible image of the company builds loyalty with customers who identify with the values of the company — such customers are more loyal to the company than to its products. Even when buying green products, consumers may gravitate toward buying from companies that best walk-the-talk on sustainability at a corporate level.

There are many ways a company can improve its image as a responsible corporate citizen. It can lighten its carbon footprint by using less energy from fossil fuels. It can conserve water to ensure the most precious natural resource on the planet is available for future generations. It can enforce strict sustainability standards for suppliers. It can be a better steward of its waste. It can "green" its buildings. It can respect employees and support communities.

These are all company-level initiatives. The company is still producing the same products, but it has improved its overall track record and polished its image as an entity that cares about society's environmental and social challenges. Consumers who share those concerns are more inclined to do business with kindred corporate spirits.

Within the last three years there has been growing evidence that a company's sustainability image is important in the B2B sector as well. In 2010, Walmart's bellwether 15-question survey of its 100,000 suppliers (see Figure 2.2) was a clear signal that the sustainability of a company's operations makes a difference to its corporate customers.

Suppliers can capitalize on this huge B2B market if their operations and products satisfy their business customers' sustainability criteria, especially if their competitors' do not. As a company pays attention to the life-cycle footprints of its products and reduces its social and environmental impacts, it earns the right to be retained as a valued member of its current customers' sustainable supply chains. If competitors are dropped from their customers' supply chains because they are sustainability laggards, more sustainable companies can pick up that business.

Gaining B2C and B2B revenue from a more responsible brand is the first of three ways that sustainability strategies bolster revenue. Next, we'll look at new revenue from new green products.

FIGURE 2.2

Walmart's Supplier Sustainability Index

Energy and Climate

1. Have you measured your corporate greenhouse gas emissions (GHGs)?
2. Have you opted to report your GHGs to the Carbon Disclosure Project (CDP)?
3. What is your total annual GHGs reported in the most recent year measured?
4. Have you set publicly available GHG reduction targets? What are they?

Material Efficiency

1. What is the total amount of solid waste from facilities that produce product(s) for Walmart in the most recent year measured?
2. Have you set publicly available solid waste reduction targets? What are they?
3. What is the total water use from facilities that produce product(s) for Walmart?
4. Have you set publicly available water use reduction targets? What are they?

Natural Resources

1. Have you established public sustainability purchasing guidelines for your direct supplier(s)?
2. Have you obtained third-party certifications for any of the products that you sell to Walmart?

People and Community

1. Do you know the location of all the facilities that produce your product(s)?
2. Do you evaluate the quality of, and capacity for, production at all supplier facilities?
3. Do you have a process for managing social compliance at the manufacturing level?
4. Do you have a process for managing social compliance with your supply base to resolve compliance issues?
5. Do you invest in community development in markets you source from/operate within?

Source: "Supplier Index" [accessed July 30, 2011], walmartstores.com/sustainability/.

New Revenue from New Green Products

The sustainability attributes of a company's products are differentiators to B2C and B2B customers who seek "green" solutions.

Figures 2.3 and 2.4 show the consumer demand for green products is still strong, although surveys indicate that consumers will not pay much extra for them. However, by applying creative approaches to manufacturing and design, environmentally friendlier products need not be more expensive or lower in quality. When green and non-green products achieve price equity, there is evidence that consumers choose the greener one. Green products may also open up new markets, as shown in the top right-hand quadrant of Figure 1.2.

There are parallel B2B revenue opportunities. GE is the classic example of a company determined to dominate the B2B market for green products. As explained by GE's ecomagination 2009 annual report, the ecomagination portfolio of products and services, which includes "green" appliances, aviation, energy, healthcare, lighting, oil and gas, transportation, and water products, grew from 15 in 2005 to over 90 by 2009.[1] When GE first launched its ecomagination thrust in 2005, it quickly generated 6.4% of the company's sales — $10.1 billion toward GE's overall revenue of $157.2 billion in 2005. Four years later, GE's ecomagination revenues had grown to $18 billion, even in a challenging global environment, and accounted for about 10% of GE's revenue. In 2011, GE pledged that ecomagination revenue will grow at twice the rate of total company revenue between 2010 and 2015, making ecomagination an even larger proportion of total company sales.

Siemens has a similar aggressive green product strategy. Its environmental portfolio includes products used in renewable energy; power transmission and distribution; green solutions for transportation; building technologies; lighting; environmental technologies; and healthcare. In fiscal year 2010, Siemens' environmental portfolio accounted for around €28 billion, or 37%, of the company's total revenue of €76 billion.[2]

Siemens and GE want to be the go-to companies for green products in their market sectors. Companies like them thrive on the upper-left-hand quadrant of Figure 1.2. They "creatively destruct" their own product lines to produce exciting new green products before their competitors do.

We have looked at two ways in which sustainability strategies can boost the top line. Next, we'll look at a third sustainability-enabled revenue stream.

FIGURE 2.3

US Consumer Intent to Buy Green

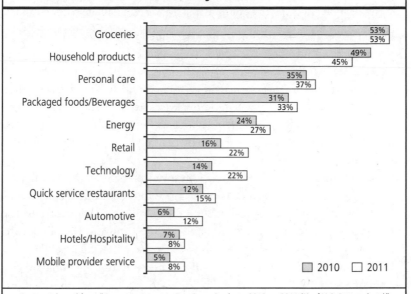

Category	2010	2011
Groceries	53%	53%
Household products	49%	45%
Personal care	35%	37%
Packaged foods/Beverages	31%	33%
Energy	24%	27%
Retail	16%	22%
Technology	14%	22%
Quick service restaurants	12%	15%
Automotive	6%	12%
Hotels/Hospitality	7%	8%
Mobile provider service	5%	8%

Source: Adapted from "Consumer Intent to Buy Green Products, 2010 vs. 2011 (% of U.S. Respondents)" [accessed July 30, 2011], EnvironmentalLeader.com/charts. Based on Cohn & Wolfe survey, June 2011.

FIGURE 2.4

"Green" US Consumer Trends

- **80% say they are still buying green products and services.**
  (Based on 2009 study by Opinion Research Corp.)

- **34% say they are more likely to buy environmentally responsible products today; another 44% indicate their environmental shopping habits have not changed.**
  (Based on 2009 Cone Consumer Environmental Survey)

- **40% say they bought products or services because they liked the social or political values of the company.**
  (Based on 2009 poll by *Time* magazine, in the midst of a recession)

- **77% of consumers describe themselves as "green" and say they are living their lives conscious of their health and environment; 57% say they made a green purchase in the past 6 months.**
  (Based on 2009 survey by Yahoo!)

Source: Joel Makower, "Green Consumers' Irrational Exuberance" [accessed July 30, 2011], GreenBiz.com. The source for each trend is shown below the finding.

New Revenue from Services and Leasing

There are four new revenue streams that companies exploit when they focus on selling services instead of producing goods that deplete natural capital.

- **Lease the product instead of selling it.** Value is delivered as a flow of services. For example, InterfaceFLOR's Evergreen Lease® system, described in Figure 2.5, leases flooring rather than selling it. A company that leases products will take them back at the end of their useful lives and recycle their components. The steady flow of monthly lease payments stabilizes the peaks and valleys of income from more volatile sales. Leasing also reduces the need to maintain manufacturing capacity to meet peak demand, another source of waste and risk.

  Interestingly, leasing reverses the motivation behind the throw-away society. Instead of using planned obsolescence to boost sales, manufacturers are encouraged to make more durable and easily upgradeable products. The longer the product lasts, the more profit for the company. Happily for the environment, longer durability avoids waste and overflowing landfill sites.

- **Use economies of scale to provide off-site outsourcing for non-core customer functions.** An example of this approach is computer companies that provide computing services for companies which previously had their own in-house IT departments.

- **Grow revenue by creatively supplementing current product revenue with associated contract services.** Think of this as a kind of onsite outsourcing. The focus of differentiation shifts to bundled services and providing end-use value while ensuring cradle-to-cradle product stewardship. For example, under the Pay-As-Painted program, Chrysler contracts out its in-plant paint shop to its paint supplier, PPG. Chrysler pays PPG a fixed amount for each vehicle that leaves the paint shop with a finish that meets Chrysler's performance quality expectations.[3] Chemical companies use this approach to sell chemical performance instead of chemicals — see the description of Dow Chemical's CHEMAWARE program in Figure 2.5.

- **Package homegrown expertise and open up a consulting practice and new revenue stream.** For example, using its 15 years of experience applying sustainability in competitive global markets, Interface offers practical guidance to other companies through its InterfaceRAISE consulting practice. The VeriGreen example in Figure 2.5 is similar.

So companies benefit from leasing, outsourcing, contracting, and consulting revenue streams, while the environment benefits from less waste and resource depletion.

FIGURE 2.5

Examples of Leasing and Services Revenue Streams

InterfaceFLOR's Evergreen Lease® system allows customers to choose from the complete range of InterfaceFLOR products, but rather than buying the floor covering, customers pay a monthly leasing charge. In return, Interface-FLOR supplies and installs its carpet tiles, replacing worn tiles as necessary.

Source: "Leasing: Convenient, Cost-Effective and Sustainable"
[accessed July 30, 2011], InterfaceFLOR.eu.

Dow Chemical's CHEMAWARE program supports the concept of chemical leasing — a complete shift in paradigm. Using this innovative system, companies can drastically increase their efficiency (up to 80% reduction in solvent use) while seeing emissions decrease. This is possible because customers are charged per square meter of product cleaned or by time needed to clean the parts. Therefore, the supplier "leases" the product and also sells a service, providing a win-win situation for all parties.

Source: "SAFECHEM Launches CHEMAWARE™ Knowledge Platform" press release
[accessed July 30, 2011], Dow.com.

VeriForm's "greening experiences" with its metal fabrication process in 2007–8 helped it launch an independently owned energy management company, VeriGreen, to advise companies on how real-world, practical solutions can quickly reduce energy costs and increase profits.

Source: "Our Experience Makes Going Green Profitable" [accessed July 30, 2011], VeriGreen.ca.

Potential Top-Line Totals

Figures 2.6 and 2.7 show the contributions to Sam's Solutions and M&D Corp. from three revenue streams.

1. **More B2C and B2B revenue from a more sustainable brand.** The 5% growth in revenue over three to five years resulting from a more sustainable company image is a conservative estimate. It is driven by the reputation of the company as an environmentally and socially responsible corporate citizen. A company can quickly improve its overall energy, water, and waste footprints, and its social responsibility track record, through continuous improvement techniques when it decides to embark on its sustainability journey, as illustrated in Figure 1.18. Reaping the low-hanging fruit of eco-efficiencies to save expenses has the co-benefit of greening the company image. All these dynamics could easily produce more than 5% additional revenue by the fifth year.

2. **New revenue from new green products.** This benefit is reaped in Stage 3.2, when the company invests research and development (R&D) dollars to create new eco-effective products. The additional revenue generated by the new green products easily recovers the R&D investment. For example, GE invested $1.5 billion on ecomagination R&D in 2009; in 2010 it committed an additional $10 billion to ecomagination R&D over the next three to five years — $2 billion per year.[4] As described above, GE is earning 10% of its revenue from new green products. Siemens is earning 37%. The assumed 2% revenue gain from new green products is a very low-ball number for Sam's Solutions and M&D Corp., allowing time to launch the new products and build a new customer base.

3. **New revenue from services and leasing.** When products are leased instead of sold, they become accessible to customers who could not otherwise finance their purchase. As the company builds a base of stable revenue from customers' lease payments, it can add creative value-added service, consulting, and support offerings. A conservative 2% increase in revenue from the leasing/service part of the business is assumed, which again allows time for the orderly launch of the new lines of business in the five-year timeframe.

Given the three revenue contributors for Sam's Solutions and M&D Corp. in Figures 2.6 and 2.7, we can conservatively assume they generate just 9% more revenue by the fifth year from their sustainability efforts. That is not a big percentage, but it is big bucks. However, not all of this flows to the profit line. We assume that new revenue reaches the bottom line in the same proportion as today's revenue does.

FIGURE 2.6

Sam's Solutions' Potential Increased Revenue

Revenue today		$1,000,000
Opportunities for Increased Revenue	*Percentage Increase in 3 to 5 Years*	*Additional Revenue*
More B2C and B2B revenue from a more sustainable brand	5%	$50,000
New revenue from new green products	2%	$20,000
New revenue from services and leasing	2%	$20,000
Increased revenue in 3 to 5 years	**9%**	**$90,000**

FIGURE 2.7

M&D Corp.'s Potential Increased Revenue

Revenue today		$500,000,000
Opportunities for Increased Revenue	*Percentage Increase in 3 to 5 Years*	*Additional Revenue*
More B2C and B2B revenue from a more sustainable brand	5%	$25,000,000
New revenue from new green products	2%	$10,000,000
New revenue from services and leasing	2%	$10,000,000
Increased revenue in 3 to 5 years	**9%**	**$45,000,000**

Reduced Energy Expenses

The profits from saving electricity could be increased even further if compa-nies also incorporated the best off-the-shelf improvements into their building structure and their office, heating, cooling, and other equipment. Overall, such changes could cut national electricity consumption by at least 75% and produce returns of around 100% a year on the investments made.

— Paul Hawken, Amory B. Lovins, and L. Hunter Lovins,
"A Road Map for Natural Capitalism"

The Lowest-Hanging Fruit

E ven if a company does not really care about the environment per se, there are substantial savings to be derived by using less energy, water, and materials in the manufacturing process. These are the "low-hanging fruit" of eco-efficiency associated with sustainability programs.

The quickest and most cost-effective way to save money is to reduce unnecessary energy use. Energy savings are the lowest-hanging eco-efficiency fruit for businesses of any size. They drive fast and significant expense reductions, are eligible for government incentives, and enhance public image. By implementing energy efficiency measures, the United States could avoid wasting $300 billion each year. In *Natural Capitalism*, Paul Hawken, Amory B. Lovins, and L. Hunter Lovins cite examples of high-tech chip-making plants that have reduced their energy use by half or more, with after-tax returns of 100% on retrofit investments. One large Asian chip-assembly plant cut its energy bills by 69% per chip in less than a year; a Singapore chip-making plant cut its energy use per wafer by 60%, with half the payback appearing within 12 months and four-fifths within 18 months; another saved $5.8 million per year from $0.7 million in retrofit projects.[1] Energy savings at IBM and Veriform are outlined in Figures 1.19 and 3.9, respectively. Further examples of energy savings at a metal fabrication company and the United States Postal Service are shown in Figure 3.1.

It is easy to improve the energy efficiency of a facility with little expertise or money. A company can capitalize on myriad proven, simple, low-risk, high-return, energy-efficiency actions, many of which require little or no capital investment. If resources permit, undertaking a comprehensive energy audit and efficiency program — with the assistance of an outside consultant if needed — may yield even greater savings.

Deloitte's reSources 2011 survey polled 400 business decision makers responsible for their companies' energy policies. It found that 90% of companies have set specific goals for their electricity and energy management, and 76% have or are setting goals to reduce electricity cost and consumption. Companies are targeting, on average, a 25% reduction in their energy consumption or cost, often within a two- to three-year time horizon. The survey also found that 71% have set or are in the process of setting goals for improving buildings' energy efficiency, and 56% of companies have or will have goals that aim to improve profitability by reducing electricity use.[2] The word is out.

FIGURE 3.1

Energy Savings Examples

Metal fabrication company: "Recently, the owner of a Canadian niche-market metal fabrication company talked with me about how and why he was focusing on becoming more energy efficient. A decade ago, energy costs represented eight percent of his sales, he said. About two years ago, energy costs as a percentage of sales had more than tripled. 'You don't have to do the math to see the challenge we faced,' he said ... 'Going green' was not the primary driver behind the decision [to be more energy efficient]: 'I did it for survival,' he said bluntly."

Source: "Shifting Markets, Shifting Mindsets: Creating Value through Cleaner and Greener Manufacturing," RBC Royal Bank and Canadian Manufacturers and Exporters, November 2010, p. 2. The quote is from the introductory welcome statement by Jayson Myers, president and CEO, Canadian Manufacturers and Exporters.

US Postal Service (USPS): USPS reduced facility energy use by 29.4%, or 9.9 trillion BTUs, from 2003 to 2010, and accumulated over $400 million in avoided energy costs from 2007 to 2010. The Morgan mail processing and distribution facility in New York City saved more than $1 million in energy costs in two years. Its green roof reduced energy use by 40% in the first year it was in place. In its Annual Sustainability Report for 2010, USPS reported a 132.7% increase in postal vehicle alternative fuel use from 2005, beating a 10% per year goal for 2015.

Source: "USPS Saves $400m on Energy Since FY2007" [accessed July 30, 2011], EnvironmentalLeader.com.

Saving Energy in Buildings: An Inside Job

In the United States, buildings account for 72% of electricity consumption, 39% of energy use, and 38% of all carbon dioxide emissions.[3] Sustainability champions look for energy savings in buildings for the same reason that "Slick Willie" Sutton robbed banks: that's where the money is.

Although many developers assume green buildings must cost more to build, green design can actually *decrease* construction costs, chiefly by reducing infrastructure expenses and by using passive heating and cooling techniques that make costly mechanical equipment unnecessary. Paul Hawken claims that 90% of the energy used in American buildings could be saved by using state-of-the-art technologies — fans, lights, pumps, super-efficient windows, motors, and other products with proven track records — combined with intelligent mechanical and building design.[4]

Using the seven approaches listed in Figure 3.2, some buildings already achieve net-zero energy. The US Department of Energy (DOE) defines a net-zero energy building (NZEB) as one that annually produces an amount of renewable power that is at least equivalent to the amount of energy it uses. The Rocky Mountain Institute, high in the snow-covered mountains of Colorado, uses passive solar heat for 99% of its heating.[5] As of May 2011, eight buildings in the United States were registered as NZEBs with the DOE, including a TD Bank location in Fort Lauderdale, FL, that is 100% powered by 400 onsite solar panels.[6]

New energy-efficient buildings are no longer a technical challenge. We also know how to retrofit old buildings to save enormous amounts of energy. In *Factor Four,* Amory Lovins describes how old wooden-frame buildings, glass-walled office towers, university buildings, and masonry row houses can be retrofitted to save 70% to 90% of their energy consumption, with the payback occurring within months or a few years.[7] In 2009, Canadian Tire saved approximately $6 million in annualized energy savings after retrofitting 361 stores with more energy-efficient lighting; the company expected to save an additional $12 million in 2010.[8]

As shown in Figure 3.3, heating, ventilation, and air-conditioning (HVAC) systems account for about 23% of energy use in commercial buildings. Every degree of heating and cooling can increase energy consumption by up to 10%.[9] Lighting accounts for just over 25% of energy use in commercial buildings. Installing readily available, proven lighting technologies can reduce a building's energy use by 50% to 70%. It is easy to do and it pays back quickly — no wonder it is called the low-hanging fruit.

FIGURE 3.2

Achieving Energy Efficiency in Buildings

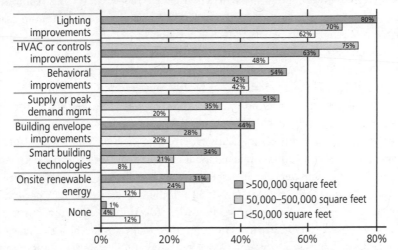

Lighting improvements — 80%, 70%, 62%
HVAC or controls improvements — 75%, 63%, 48%
Behavioral improvements — 54%, 42%, 42%
Supply or peak demand mgmt — 51%, 35%, 20%
Building envelope improvements — 44%, 28%, 20%
Smart building technologies — 34%, 21%, 8%
Onsite renewable energy — 31%, 24%, 12%
None — 1%, 4%, 12%

■ >500,000 square feet
□ 50,000–500,000 square feet
□ <50,000 square feet

0%   20%   40%   60%   80%

Source: Adapted from "Energy Efficiency Indicator: 2011 Global Results," Johnson Controls' Institute for Building Efficiency, June 2011, p. 13. Based on a worldwide survey of 4,000 building owners and managers.

FIGURE 3.3

Energy Use in Commercial Buildings

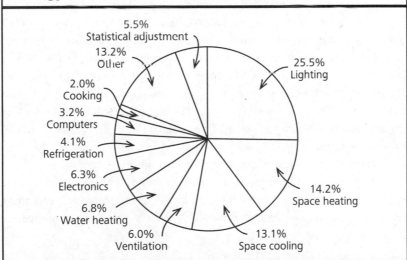

5.5% Statistical adjustment
13.2% Other
2.0% Cooking
3.2% Computers
4.1% Refrigeration
6.3% Electronics
6.8% Water heating
6.0% Ventilation
25.5% Lighting
14.2% Space heating
13.1% Space cooling

Source: Adapted from Environmental Leader ."Primary Energy Use in US Commercial Buildings (% of total)" in *Environmental and Energy Data Book Q2 2011*, July 2011, p.15. Based on Urban Land Institute data, 2010.

Computing Energy Savings in IT

Computers can help save energy when they are used to monitor and control HVAC systems in buildings, or when people replace travel and commuting with telepresence technologies. On the other hand, enormous amounts of energy are required to power and cool corporate computer server farms, and PCs and monitors consume 31% of all energy used by IT equipment.

Between July 2009 and January 2010, QDI Strategies did a study of over 110,000 PCs across a broad sample of North American industries and companies of different sizes. It found that desktop PCs are "On" more than 90% of the time, day and night, and fewer than 10% of computers are configured to take advantage of energy-saving features. However, QDI also found that automated, centralized PC power-management tools can save an organization with 1,000 desktop computers nearly $24,000 annually.[10] PC power management is helping GE and Dell boast savings of $2.5 million and $1.8 million per year, respectively. They also benefit by a substantial reduction in CO_2 emissions.[11]

So why isn't every IT department doing this? Many are, but historically very few IT departments were accountable for the data center's electricity bills or the electricity bills for the hundreds or thousands of computers scattered throughout the organization. They had no incentive to pay attention to the energy efficiency of these networks, since the bills were charged to the real estate facilities department. Why would overburdened IT staff concern themselves with energy efficiencies when another department got the financial benefit?

Times change. CFOs and CEOs now mandate that IT departments are responsible for the energy used by their systems, and the compensation of CIO and IT professionals is tied to cutting electricity use. Not surprisingly, they are now looking at innovative approaches. A 2011 study sponsored by the Carbon Disclosure Project found that US businesses with annual revenues of more than $1 billion can achieve energy savings of $12.3 billion a year by 2020.[12] The examples in Figure 3.4 show how Lockheed Martin, the US Department of Energy, and Intel save energy in their IT functions using consolidation, virtualization, and cloud computing.

Further, real-time systems help companies monitor and optimize the HVAC systems throughout buildings so they can reap energy savings from all systems in the building, not just what belongs to IT. IT departments have leapt from being disinterested spectators in the energy efficiency game to being captains of the team.

FIGURE 3.4

Examples of Energy Savings in IT

Lockheed: Lockheed Martin's campaign to embed sustainability into its operations has driven down the company's energy costs for its IT systems, which are central to the firm's business. Between 2007 and 2010 the company consolidated 4,000 data servers, a move that led to a savings of 26-million kWh of electricity and $2.6 million in annual costs.

Source: Leslie Guevarra, "Lockheed Saves $2.6M in IT Energy Costs; Tops Water, Waste Targets" [accessed July 30, 2011], GreenBiz.com, April 20, 2011.

Department of Energy: "Companies should consider ways to reduce the number of data servers to minimize electricity costs and free up office space. The U.S. Department of Energy collapsed 13 data servers into two. This project freed up nearly 3,000 sq. feet of office space, reduced data center energy usage by 50 percent and saved $1 million in operating costs."

Source: David Constable, "Reaching the Crossroads of Corporate Sustainability and Strong Business Practices" [accessed July 30, 2011], EnvironmentalLeader.com.

Intel: Intel plans to save $25 billion by 2015 through energy-efficient IT initiatives, including the use of cloud computing.

Source: "Intel Plans $25bn Efficiency Saving" [accessed July 30, 2011], EnvironmentalLeader.com.

Driving Energy Savings in Transportation

Companies pay shipping costs for their raw materials and/or their finished goods. If companies do not cover transportation costs overtly, they usually are buried in the buying or selling price. That means companies are looking for ways to reduce the amount of fuel used in transportation, even if they do not have their own company fleet of cars or trucks. Savings in resource-efficient transportation and shipping are achieved through:

- Reduced fuel costs from more efficient modes of transportation
- Increased cost-effectiveness due to lighter, smaller, and more efficiently packaged products
- Fewer vehicles or loads due to smarter combinations of shipments by batching loads
- More efficient routing algorithms

We are primarily concerned with the first option here.

For a company like Chiquita, which sells fresh fruit and vegetables, the price of bunker fuel is an important variable component of its transportation costs. As they have for most companies, Chiquita's fuel costs have increased substantially in recent years. It offsets the effect of these increases through fuel surcharges, and mitigates the effect of fluctuating fuel prices by purchasing bunker fuel forward contracts that lock in fuel prices for up to 75% of its expected core shipping needs for up to three years. In addition, diesel fuel and other transportation costs are significant components of what Chiquita spends on the produce it purchases from growers and distributors. If the price of any of these items increases significantly, there is no assurance that Chiquita will be able to pass on those increases to its customers. The price of fuel is critical to such companies.

As Figure 3.5 shows, many shipping companies are willing to put time and effort into sustainability, even if there is no return on investment (ROI), while 11% of retail and third-party logistics shippers want a considerable ROI. Danish shipping company Maersk Line plans to build a fleet of container ships that it describes as the world's largest and most energy efficient. Maersk's new fleet will use smaller engines, a waste-heat recovery system, and economy of scale to achieve its fuel savings.[13] The fleet will also use 35% less fuel per container than thousands of ships being delivered to Maersk's competitors, transforming fuel consumption used in transportation into a competitive advantage.

We have looked at saving energy in buildings, IT, and transportation. Next we look at generating energy onsite, as suggested by Figure 3.6.

FIGURE 3.5

Shippers' Position on Sustainability

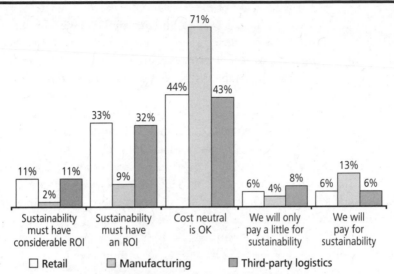

	Sustainability must have considerable ROI	Sustainability must have an ROI	Cost neutral is OK	We will only pay a little for sustainability	We will pay for sustainability
Retail	11%	33%	44%	6%	6%
Manufacturing	2%	9%	71%	4%	13%
Third-party logistics	11%	32%	43%	8%	6%

☐ Retail   ▨ Manufacturing   ▨ Third-party logistics

Source: Adapted from Environmental Leader, "Shippers Position on Sustainability Investments (% of respondents)" in *Environmental and Energy Data Book Q2 2011,* July 2011, p.48. Based on American Shipper data, February 2011.

FIGURE 3.6

From Energy Expense to Revenue

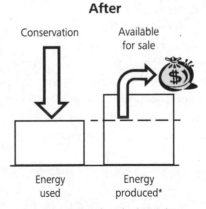

Before

Energy used   Energy produced

After

Conservation   Available for sale

Energy used   Energy produced*

*Co-generation, geothermal, solar, wind, etc.

Renewing Energy Savings with Substitutions

Figure 3.6 shows companies the benefits of conserving energy while generating their own. The sequence of these efforts is important: "reduce before you produce." Companies are discovering amazing opportunities for energy savings and are driving down their energy requirements. That makes them good candidates for the other part of the energy pincer movement illustrated in the figure: they can create renewable energy onsite for their remaining energy requirements.

Renewable energy alternatives are becoming more cost competitive. In 2011, wind power was down to 4.2 cents/kWh, making it competitive with traditional non-renewable energy sources. The photovoltaic (PV) industry is reducing the cost of solar energy at a breakneck rate. Prices on solar panels have dropped over 50% in just two years. The US Department of Energy said in February 2011 that it would spend $27 million on a new "sun shot" effort to reduce the cost of solar power by 75% by 2020 in a bid to make the renewable power source as cheap as fossil fuels — about 6 cents/kWh.[14] If the cost of PV energy achieves par with conventional sources, it will continue flourishing even if government incentives are withdrawn.

Other renewable energy projects that seemed unprofitable two years ago are beginning to look good from an ROI perspective. Companies use combined heat and power (CHP) technologies to capture wasted heat from their industrial processes and use it to generate electricity. The company can use the resulting power onsite and feed excess electricity into the electrical grid to generate a credit on the company's bill from the local electrical utility. For example, Campbell's makes both soup and electricity from the steam in its cookers, and generates revenue from both.

It would be nice if the billions of dollars in fossil fuel subsidies were converted to support for renewable energy. To help cover the price differential in the meantime, there are government incentive programs available from most levels of government in most jurisdictions. They include grants, tax breaks, loan guarantees, and technical assistance for green building and renewable-energy components of commercial, residential, and industrial projects. Additional financial and technical assistance may be available from utilities, nonprofits, and faith-based organizations.

As shown in Figures 3.7 and 3.8, companies are already finding ways to generate green power and reduce energy needs. Incentive programs usually build momentum and then are withdrawn once the technology matures. Smart companies capitalize on financial support packages before their competitors do and enjoy a first-mover advantage.

FIGURE 3.7

Top 10 Onsite Generators

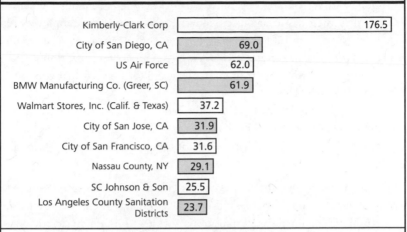

Kimberly-Clark Corp	176.5
City of San Diego, CA	69.0
US Air Force	62.0
BMW Manufacturing Co. (Greer, SC)	61.9
Walmart Stores, Inc. (Calif. & Texas)	37.2
City of San Jose, CA	31.9
City of San Francisco, CA	31.6
Nassau County, NY	29.1
SC Johnson & Son	25.5
Los Angeles County Sanitation Districts	23.7

Source: Adapted from Environmental Leader, "Top 10 On-Site Green Power Generation (Annual Green Power Usage of EPA Green Power Partners [kWh millions])" in *Environmental and Energy Data Book Q2 2011*, July 2011, p.9. Based on EPA Green Power Partnership data, April 2011.

FIGURE 3.8

Companies with Energy Cost Reduction Goals

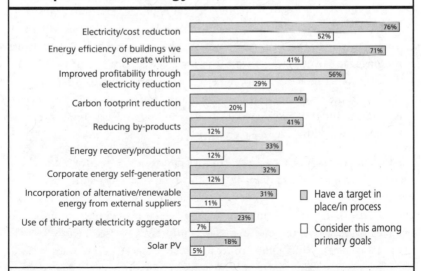

	Have a target in place/in process	Consider this among primary goals
Electricity/cost reduction	76%	52%
Energy efficiency of buildings we operate within	71%	41%
Improved profitability through electricity reduction	56%	29%
Carbon footprint reduction	n/a	20%
Reducing by-products	41%	12%
Energy recovery/production	33%	12%
Corporate energy self-generation	32%	12%
Incorporation of alternative/renewable energy from external suppliers	31%	11%
Use of third-party electricity aggregator	23%	7%
Solar PV	18%	5%

Source: Adapted from "Electricity and Cost Reduction Goals of Business, June 2011 (% of respondents)" [accessed August 30, 2011], EnvironmentalLeader.com/charts. Based on Deloitte and Harrison Group report, May 2011.

The Secret Sauce of Eco-Efficiency Savings: Engaged Employees

Educated, caring employees can make a critical difference to energy conservation in their day-to-day discretionary activities at work. Employees can save energy by turning off lights when they leave offices and conference rooms, using stairs instead of elevators when going up or down a few floors, using the power-saving settings on their computers, and turning off their computers when they are out of the office.

Encouraging employees, especially the purchasing department, to use systems thinking helps them see how long-term operational costs are much more significant than one-time purchase prices for things like transformers, wire, and motors.

- It is more energy efficient and more cost effective to spend more money to acquire efficient transformers and then save money on energy. Purchasing cheap, inefficient distribution transformers wastes $1 billion in electricity per year in the United States.[15]
- Electricians usually bid the thinnest and cheapest allowable wire to save money on materials. The irony is that if lighting circuits used fatter wire with less electrical resistance, lower electricity bills would generate after-tax returns of 193%.[16]
- Pumping is the most common application for motors, and motors use 75% of all industrial electricity.[17] Manufacturing requires motors and pumps — lots of them. Interface Inc. discovered that using big straight pipes with small pumps, instead of small crooked pipes with big pumps, cost less, even before the ongoing energy savings from the lower electricity use of the smaller pumps, motors, motor controls, and electrical components. By first laying out the pipe route and then positioning the tanks, boilers, and other connected equipment, Interface discovered it could use 7-horsepower pumps instead of 95-horsepower pumps, a 92% reduction.[18]

Turned-on employees, energized by an opportunity to reduce the environmental footprint of their company, astound their managers with good ideas. Figure 3.9 gives a few examples of how technology-based ideas can provide fast and substantial returns on investment. Add "green teams" into the mix, and behavior-based eco-savings are even more impressive — see Figure 8.19 for examples of green teams' efforts to reduce waste expenses. Employees' innovative ideas, firsthand knowledge of work flows, and passion to help the company solve its sustainability puzzle are the underpinnings of eco-efficiency savings. Engaged employees trump technology.

FIGURE 3.9

Energy Savings at VeriForm

VeriForm, a steel fabricating company located in Cambridge, Ontario, invested $46,186 between 2006 and 2008 to reduce electricity costs by more than 58% ($89,152 annually) and increase its profit by 76%. The average payback period for its 42 energy saving projects was 6.3 months. As can be seen from the table of projects below, some projects paid for themselves in just weeks. The company also reduced its natural gas consumption by 90% and its CO_2 emissions by over 45% annually.

Project	Initial Cost (Can$)	Annual Savings (Can$)	Payback Period (Years)
Replace HID plant lighting with T5 lights in the old plant ($6,000) and in the new, expanded area ($2,000)	$8,000*	$20,916	0.38 (4.5 months)
Install equipment capacitors to raise power factor to above 90 to avoid surcharge on electrical bill for inefficiencies	$11,285	$24,118	0.46 (5.5 months)
Install a single tamper-resistant, programmable thermostat in the plant to replace multiple manual thermostats	$1,200	$13,911	0.08 (1 month)
Install wire heating disconnects on five bay doors so when the bay door goes up, the heat turns off in the whole shop (This encourages staff to chase shippers to unload faster)	$1,200	$7,893	0.15 (1.8 months)
Turn off printers/monitors/ computers at night	$250	$2,978	0.08 (1 month)
Install software to print multiple pages per sheet	$320	$1,200	0.26 (3.1 months)

* An additional $1,000 grant from the local electricity utility helped defray the initial cost. All other projects listed were self-financed, without any assistance from subsidies or grants.

Source: "Manufacturer Finds Lighting Energy Efficiency Convenient, Truthfully" [accessed July 30, 2011], GreenManufacturer.net.

Potential Energy Expense Savings

Despite the primary focus on energy savings in many companies these days, energy costs are still only a small fraction of total costs in most industries (a conservative estimate is that the cost of electricity and fuel represents 2% of company revenue, although this amount is growing as the cost of energy increases). As a result, executives may not pay them the attention they should. They forget that energy savings go straight to the bottom line, whereas only 5% to 15% of revenue typically does. That is, you'd need about 7 to 20 times the value of energy savings in additional revenue to generate the same amount of profit. If you were the CEO, would you rather improve profit by saving $100,000 on your energy bill or by somehow generating $2,000,000 more revenue?

In *Factor Four*, the authors propose that resource and energy use be improved by a factor of four.[19] That is, companies can generate twice the output with half the input of materials and energy; or four times the output with the same amount of materials and energy; or the same amount of output with 25% of the materials and energy. The authors of *Natural Capitalism* describe the "Factor Ten Club," which is committed to reducing material and energy intensity by a factor of 10 — a 90% reduction in energy and materials, rather than the 75% reduction proposed by *Factor Four*.[20]

Some companies already save over 100% of their energy bill. How? If a company can generate more energy onsite than is required for its internal use, in some jurisdictions it can sell the excess power back to the grid, as suggested in Figure 3.7. The resulting revenue is counted within these energy savings. Similarly, if a cap-and-trade system is implemented in the company's operational jurisdictions, any revenue from carbon credits the company is able to create and sell would also contribute to energy savings.

Using the approaches outlined in this chapter, we conservatively assume a Factor Four improvement in energy productivity for Sam's Solutions and M&D Corp. That is, the companies use today's best practices and technologies to reduce electricity and fuel costs by 75% within the next three to five years. If technologies improve, the savings accelerate. Figures 3.10 and 3.11 show the total energy savings. In the Conclusion we discuss ways to cover the up-front costs of any sustainability project, although impressive payback periods and ROIs, like those shown for energy-saving initiatives at VeriForm in Figure 3.9, are possible for very little cost.

FIGURE 3.10

Sam's Solutions' Reduced Energy Expenses

Cost of energy today	$20,000
Assumption: Factor Four (75%) savings on energy used for lighting, heating and cooling, pumps and motors, IT, green buildings, employee actions, transportation, renewable energy substitutions, etc.; includes any revenue from selling excess energy back to the grid and from selling carbon credits	75%
Reduced energy expenses in 3 to 5 years	$15,000

FIGURE 3.11

M&D Corp.'s Reduced Energy Expenses

Cost of energy today	$10,000,000
Assumption: Factor Four (75%) savings on energy used for lighting, heating and cooling, pumps and motors, IT, green buildings, employee actions, transportation, renewable energy substitutions, etc.; includes any revenue from selling excess energy back to the grid and from selling carbon credits	75%
Reduced energy expenses in 3 to 5 years	$7,500,000

BENEFIT 3

Reduced Waste Expenses

I'm told that less than 3% of the throughput of the entire
industrial system has any value six months afterward.
We industrialists operate a waste-making machine.

— Ray Anderson, "More Happiness, Less Stuff"

In Bed with Embedded Waste

Companies buy raw materials with the aim of turning them into marketable products. While a certain amount of the purchased material and energy ends up embodied in products, more of it ends up as "non-product output" or waste — material that was purchased and paid for but that was ultimately thrown away. If the term "waste" were replaced with "squandered corporate assets," shareholders would pressure corporations to pay more attention to this opportunity for cost savings. And the business imperative to stop squandering these assets has environmental co-benefits.

Waste is embedded in processes, a direct result of inefficient systems and procedures that are, perhaps unwittingly, designed to produce waste. Solid waste, waste water, and air emissions are indicative of production inefficiency. Process redesign saves embedded waste costs. (We will see, under Benefit 4, how dematerialization, substitution, recycling, and product take-back save materials costs and further reduce waste.)

If business leaders were asked how much material is wasted by industry each year, most would admit that a certain percentage is wasted, but not a great deal. Actually, we are more than 10 times better at wasting resources than we are at using them. A study by the US National Academy of Engineering found that about 93% of materials that companies buy and "consume" never end up in saleable products at all, as illustrated in Figure 4.1. Moreover, 80% of products are discarded after a single use, something Ray Anderson alludes to in the quote that opened this chapter.

However, it is also important to recognize that not all waste is equal. When the waste stream consists of many different materials or commodities, as in the case of food waste, the economic values and environmental footprints of the waste components can vary widely. Figure 4.2 shows the value and weights of various waste streams in a paint shop. It shows that about 39% of the value of the raw materials ends up in useful products, while the other 61% is wasted. That is still high, but more hopeful than the 12% to 88% split by weight. Since we are looking at the economics of waste reduction, we conservatively assume that 70% of the value of the company's purchased materials and water is used for products and only the remaining 30% is wasted.

In today's take-make-*waste* business model, waste has become an accepted by-product of doing business. The wake-up call comes when the costs of wasted materials, capital, and labor are added to arrive at the total cost of waste.

FIGURE 4.1

US Waste Story (by volume)

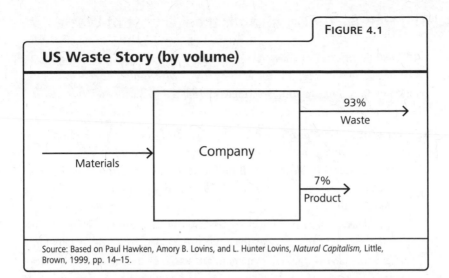

Source: Based on Paul Hawken, Amory B. Lovins, and L. Hunter Lovins, *Natural Capitalism,* Little, Brown, 1999, pp. 14–15.

FIGURE 4.2

Typical Material-Waste Stream

Material and money flows in a paint shop

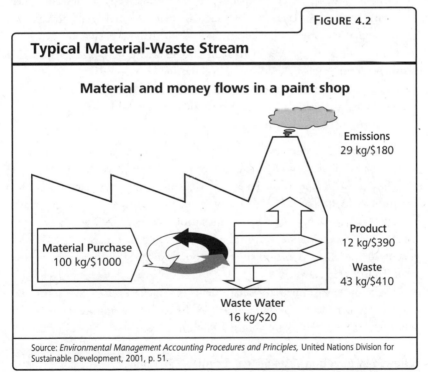

Source: *Environmental Management Accounting Procedures and Principles,* United Nations Division for Sustainable Development, 2001, p. 51.

The Four-Factor Formula for the Full Cost of Waste

Too often, the cost of waste is equated with the cost of waste handling. To more accurately account for a company's waste bill, we need to rethink waste and tally four factors described in the UN document *Environmental Management Accounting Procedures and Principles,* illustrated in Figure 4.3.[1]

1. **Cost of materials purchased but later wasted (60%).** This includes raw materials, auxiliary materials, operating materials, packaging, and water.
2. **Cost of processing the material before it is wasted (20%).** This includes the wasted energy and labor consumed working on the material before it becomes scrap.
3. **Cost of waste prevention and environmental management (10%).** This includes any external services for environmental management, personnel for general environmental management activities, research and development on waste issues, extra expenditures for cleaner technologies, and other environmental management costs such as environmental monitoring, environmental assessments and audits, and wildlife habitat protection.
4. **Cost of end-of-pipe waste treatment and waste disposal (10%).** This includes storage, haulage, disposal, and tipping fees; depreciation for related equipment; related personnel costs; any fines and penalties; insurance for environmental liabilities; and any provisions for cleanup costs, remediation, reclamation, and decommissioning.

These costs are offset by any revenue realized from selling sorted waste streams or selling new products created from previously discarded waste.

The purchase cost of wasted materials is the most important factor, accounting for 40% to 90% of the total cost of waste, depending on the value of raw materials and the labor intensity of the sector.[2] We used 60% as a mid-range assumption in our calculations in the list above and then conservatively estimated 20% as the proportion of waste costs associated with processing the material before it is wasted.

The term "environmental management" is sometimes used to refer to the third and fourth factors. In Canada in 2008 the cost of environmental management totaled $5.2 billion, up almost 10% from 2006. These expenditures were mostly directed toward waste management and sewage services ($1.6 billion), followed by pollution abatement and control ($1.3 billion).[3] The costs related purely to disposal (e.g., waste disposal fees, external waste transport) account for 1% to 2% of the *total* expenses, not just the waste costs, for a manufacturing company.[4] We estimated 10% as the proportion of waste costs for both waste prevention and waste treatment/disposal.

FIGURE 4.3

The Four Contributors to the Full Cost of Waste

1. Cost of materials purchased but later wasted   **60%**

3. Cost of waste prevention and environmental management   **10%**

2. Cost of processing materials before they are wasted   **20%**

4. Cost of waste treatment and disposal   **10%**

Waste

Company

Materials

Product

Source: Based on *Environmental Management Accounting Procedures and Principles,* United Nations Division for Sustainable Development, 2001, pp. 19 and 59.

Company Efforts to Avoid Waste

Companies in the United States dispose of 7.6 billion tons of industrial waste each year. Much of this industrial waste is made up reusable non-hazardous materials. No wonder some companies are taking aggressive measures to stop wasting their waste.

Lockheed set a goal of reducing the amount of waste sent to landfills by 25% by the close of 2012, based on 2007 levels. The targets are absolute reductions, not reductions in intensity, where consumption, waste, and emissions are typically measured in comparison to other factors such as revenue, units of production, or number of employees. By the end of the first quarter of 2011, the firm had cut waste-to-landfill by 30%, exceeding the targeted reduction.[5]

In 2010, Boeing diverted 73% of its non-hazardous solid waste from landfill, compared with 68% in 2009. From 2007 to 2010, the company's diversion rate improved 26%. In April 2011, the Boeing 787 assembly plant in North Charleston, SC, became the company's fourth zero-waste-to-landfill site and its first major commercial airplane production facility to attain "zero waste" status. Boeing's other zero-waste sites are a helicopter plant in Philadelphia, a Salt Lake City factory where commercial airplane parts are fabricated, and a strategic-missile-and-defense-systems facility in Huntsville, AL.[6]

Waste-reduction accomplishments at Procter & Gamble, Interface, and Walmart are outlined in Figure 4.4.

Continuous improvement of old manufacturing processes to prevent embedded waste eventually hits a wall when the cost of squeezing out additional waste savings exceeds the savings that would be gained. The biggest savings breakthroughs occur when companies adopt a fresh approach to process design that considers industrial systems as a whole, rather than as a collection of isolated parts. Rather than battling the law of diminishing returns while fine-tuning existing processes, designers use whole-system thinking to discover that saving a large fraction of resources can actually cost less than saving a smaller fraction of resources.

A wonderful example of replacing incremental environmental thinking with quantum leap thinking is offered by architect Bill McDonough's "no-pipe" approach. Environmentalists encourage working on "front-of-pipe" eco-efficiency instead of "end-of-pipe" compliance and filtering. McDonough goes even further and eliminates the pipe: "You put the filter in your head and design the problem out of existence."[7] The side benefit is that when there is no waste, the environment is healthier and there is no need for government regulations.

FIGURE 4.4

Examples of Savings on Waste

Procter & Gamble: In 2010, Procter & Gamble's manufacturing facility in Auburn, ME, became the company's first in North America to achieve zero-waste-to-landfill status by recycling or reusing more than 60% of the overall waste produced and incinerating the rest for energy production. The company's Global Asset Recovery Purchases (GARP) team found a beneficial use for the nearly 40% of factory waste that could not be recycled or reused. The excess materials were incinerated and used to power the facility; any excess power was sold back to the local utility. The GARP team calculated that the program diverted over 10,000 tons of waste from the landfill and saved the company tens of millions of dollars in cost recovery over the year. Auburn is the ninth P&G plant to earn the distinction of zero-waste-to-landfill, which P&G says fits its goal of having zero waste going to landfills globally and instead being beneficially reused in its value stream.

Source: "P&G Announces Its First North American Manufacturing Plant to Achieve Zero Waste to Landfill" press release [accessed July 30, 2011], PGinvestor.com, December 6, 2010.

Interface: Interface Inc. has an objective to eliminate all waste in the manufacture of carpet. This zero-waste strategy led to a corporate-wide treasure hunt under its QUEST™ program to engage employees in identifying, measuring, and eliminating waste in its manufacturing processes. As a result of employees' valuable suggestions to minimize material usage and improve the efficiency of equipment and processes, Interface achieved a 50% reduction in waste cost per unit, resulting in $372 million in avoided waste costs by 2010. Interface waste reduction efforts have resulted in a 76% decrease in total waste to landfills from its carpet factories since 1996.

Source: "Waste" [accessed July 30, 2011], Interfaceglobal.com.

Walmart: "During the recession, ... [Walmart] did not cut back on its sustainability spending at all because it is driving bottom-line benefit. [The company] has a goal of zero waste from its operations by 2025, and one Canadian store has achieved 97.6% diversion."

Source: Jim Harris, "What You Don't Know about Green Tech — But Should" [accessed July 30, 2011], Backbonemag.com, May 13, 2011.

Bonus: Revenue from Selling Waste

Each year it costs US companies $22 billion to put their waste into landfills. The materials in that landfilled waste are worth an estimated $20 billion.[8] The real waste is not the materials; it is the lost opportunity.

Valuable materials such as cardboard, boxboard, mixed paper, glass, ferrous metals, copper, aluminum, plastics, organics, and construction and demolition materials in useful concentrations are embedded in waste streams. However, most companies have limited knowledge of the composition of their waste and know even less about how to separate the marketable portion from the waste stream. Innovative services such as RecycleMatch provide marketplaces where waste can be traded as valuable raw material. The RecycleMatch website gives the following examples:

- Instead of paying $1.5 million to put used materials into a landfill, IBM found a way to sell those "waste" materials for $1.5 million, resulting in a net $3 million improvement.[9]
- GM's various recycling activities generated more than $2.5 billion in revenue between 2007 and 2010. It now earns $1 billion a year from selling scrap. That is on top of the value the company has achieved by reusing and repurposing materials within its own operations.[10]
- Recycling made the US Postal Service (USPS) $13 million in revenues last year, while saving $9.1 million in landfill fees...in 2010 it recycled more than 222,000 tons of material, almost 8,000 tons more than in 2009.[11]

Using the waste from one company as the food for another is called "industrial ecology," illustrated in Figure 4.5. One of the first examples of industrial ecology comes from Kalundborg, Denmark, where companies conveniently located near each other in the city's eco-industrial park trade various by-products: steam and heat, water, refinery gas, gypsum, biomass, liquid fertilizer, fly ash, and sludge. They invested $60 million over five years on the infrastructure to support these exchanges and have reaped over $120 million in cost savings.[12] This increased efficiency benefits the bottom lines of all participating partners.

There are eco-industrial networks across Canada, the United States, and Europe, referred to as eco-industrial parks, industrial ecosystems, zero emissions clusters, and sustainable technology parks. The closed-loop systems in these industrial ecosystems benefit the companies, the communities ... and the environment. They profit from each others' waste.

FIGURE 4.5

Industrial Ecology

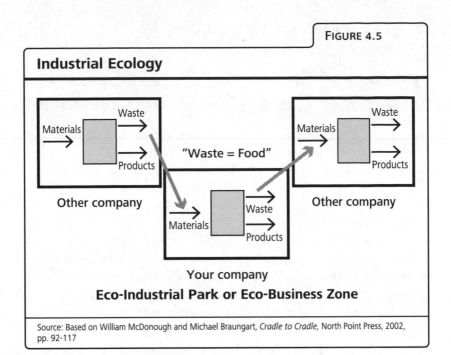

"Waste = Food"

Other company

Your company

Eco-Industrial Park or Eco-Business Zone

Source: Based on William McDonough and Michael Braungart, *Cradle to Cradle*, North Point Press, 2002, pp. 92-117

Potential Waste Savings Help Build a Sustainability Capital Reserve

The cost to industry of environmental protection, including pollution reduction, waste management, monitoring, regulatory reporting, legal fees, and insurance, has risen rapidly in the past 20 years, with increasingly stringent environmental regulations. Conventional management accounting systems attribute many of those environmental costs to general overhead accounts, with the consequence that product and production managers have no incentive to reduce environmental costs, and executives are often unaware of the extent of environmental costs.[13] When a full-cost-accounting approach is used for waste, alarm bells should ring in the C-suite.

Waste reduction makes a surprisingly high contribution to potential bottom-line benefits from sustainability strategies. As mentioned earlier, the cost of waste is often equated with the cost of waste handling and disposal. That is like saying the cost of waste on a construction site is just the cost of having the scrap lumber and wallboard hauled away in a dumpster, ignoring the cost of buying lumber and wallboard in the first place, or the cost of labor used to create and gather the waste. When we calculate the total cost of waste for Sam's Solutions (Figure 4.6) and M&D Corp. (Figure 4.7), we start with the cost of all materials and water purchased and conservatively assume that only 30% of their value is wasted, as discussed above. Working backward using the four-factor formula, we easily calculate the full cost of waste by dividing the cost of the wasted materials by 60%, which is the same as multiplying it by 1.67.

What should we assume as the potential waste reduction factor within the next three to five years? PepsiCo's UK and Ireland division has set a goal to achieve zero waste across the supply chain within 10 years.[14] Walmart's California operations have diverted more than 80% of their waste from landfills, and the retailer's goal is to create zero waste.[15] In 2010, GM announced that 52% of its worldwide facilities were landfill free, and it aimed to grow that figure continuously.[16] These are wonderfully aggressive targets.

Based on these examples, we conservatively assume only a 20% reduction in the net cost of waste, including any offsetting revenue from sales of waste or new finished products made from waste. Then we skim half the savings off the top and squirrel them away in a Sustainability Capital Reserve (which we'll explain at the end of the next chapter). We count the remaining savings as the bottom-line contributor, as shown in Figures 4.6 and 4.7. When companies plug in their own data, they will be pleasantly surprised at the upward possibilities if they decide to get serious about reducing waste.

FIGURE 4.6

Sam's Solutions' Potential Reduced Waste Expenses

Total cost of materials and water purchased	$50,000
Assumption: Percentage of materials purchased but later wasted	*30%*
Cost of materials and water purchased but later wasted	$15,000
Assumption: Percentage of the total cost of waste made up of the cost of materials purchased but later wasted	*60%*
Total cost of waste	$25,000
Assumption: Percentage of total cost of waste saved through onsite recycling/reuse, and other lean manufacturing programs; includes any revenue from selling sorted waste	*20%*
Savings of waste expenses	$5,000
Assumption: Percentage of savings on waste set aside in the Sustainability Capital Reserve for more sustainability projects	*50%*
Contribution to Sustainability Capital Reserve	$2,500
Reduced waste expenses in 3 to 5 years	$2,500

FIGURE 4.7

M&D Corp.'s Potential Reduced Waste Expenses

Total cost of materials and water purchased	$150,000,000
Assumption: Percentage of materials purchased but later wasted	*30%*
Cost of materials and water purchased but later wasted	$45,000,000
Assumption: Percentage of the total cost of waste made up of the cost of materials purchased but later wasted	*60%*
Total cost of waste	$75,000,000
Assumption: Percentage of total cost of waste saved through onsite recycling/reuse, and other lean manufacturing programs; includes any revenue from selling sorted waste	*20%*
Savings of waste expenses	$15,000,000
Assumption: Percentage of savings on waste set aside in the Sustainability Capital Reserve for more sustainability projects	*50%*
Contribution to Sustainability Capital Reserve	$7,500,000
Reduced waste expenses in 3 to 5 years	$7,500,000

BENEFIT 4

Reduced Materials and Water Expenses

Through fundamental changes in both production design and technology, farsighted companies are developing ways to make natural resources — energy, minerals, water, forests — stretch 5, 10, or even 100 times further than they do today. These major resource savings often yield higher profits than small resource savings do — or even saving no resources at all would — and not only pay for themselves over time but in many cases reduce initial capital investments.

— Paul Hawken, Amory B. Lovins, and L. Hunter Lovins,
"A Road Map for Natural Capitalism"

Saving Natural Capital Saves Financial Capital

All companies use materials. Companies that manufacture goods take raw materials and parts, which are the finished product from the supplier's raw materials, and combine them to produce finished goods for customers. Wholesale and retail companies buy materials in the form of products for resale. Commercial establishments purchase materials in the form of office consumables, especially paper, and often food for their cafeterias. Packaging materials are used in all sectors, as is water, another material.

We use the word "materials" as an umbrella term to include raw materials, parts, finished goods, consumables, packaging, and water. Materials arrive at the receiving dock or through a pipe, are processed by the company, and leave the shipping dock as finished goods for sale to another company or to be sold directly to the consumer. They also go down the sewer, up the chimney, or into the dumpster as waste. Under Benefit 3 we looked at savings opportunities involving waste. However, from a sustainability perspective, using fewer materials is even better as it minimizes the extraction and consumption of increasingly scarce natural capital. In fact, a truly sustainable enterprise would use and waste no new raw materials.

Manufacturing, construction, wholesale, and retail companies use the most materials. Material purchase costs can make up from 50% to 80% of total expenses for an American manufacturing company and 70% of expenses for its German counterpart.[1] Another study pegged the cost of materials for German manufacturers as 57% of overall expenses (see Figure 5.1).

We conservatively assume that M&D Corp.'s material and water costs are equivalent to 30% of its revenue. Services companies use fewer materials, so we estimate material costs for Sam's Solutions are only 5% of its revenue.

As illustrated in Figure 5.2, there are four ways to save money on materials.

- **Dematerialization:** Reduce the amount of material used per product to reduce the material intensity of goods.
- **Substitution:** Use less expensive, more environmentally friendly, raw materials.
- **Recycling onsite waste:** Reduce, reuse, and recycle scrap materials, turning them into useful raw materials for products instead of throwing them away.
- **Product Take-Back:** Reuse and recycle components and materials from returned products in a closed-loop, cradle-to-cradle system.

We consider each approach in this chapter.

FIGURE 5.1

Costs in Manufacturing Companies

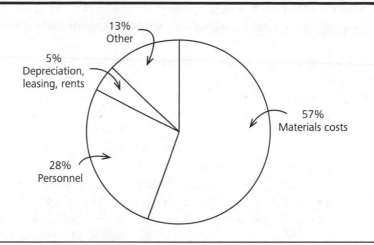

13%
Other

5%
Depreciation,
leasing, rents

57%
Materials costs

28%
Personnel

Source: Adapted from *Flow Management for Manufacturing Companies,* University of Augsberg, 2003, p. 9. Based on data for manufacturing companies in Germany.

FIGURE 5.2

Four Ways to Reduce Materials

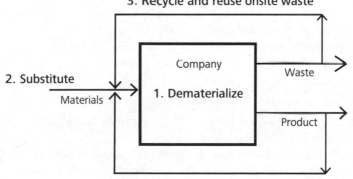

3. Recycle and reuse onsite waste

2. Substitute

Materials

Company

1. Dematerialize

Waste

Product

4. Product take-back/Cradle-to-cradle/Closed loop

Source: Based on Bob Doppelt, *The Power of Sustainable Thinking,* Earthscan, 2008, p. 34.

Savings from Dematerialization

Dematerialization is doing more with less. Using less means the company buys less. Buying less saves money. Ergo, dematerialization saves money. That is the bottom-line benefit. The sustainability-related benefit is that we raze less natural capital.

In some ways, sustainability is a reframing of traditional approaches to lean manufacturing and running an efficient organization. Dematerialization helps streamline operations and increase organizational effectiveness. Minimum-material design not only minimizes the material intensity of the finished product; it also has labor productivity benefits. There are reduced handling costs because there are fewer components or less material, and there is less over-time because of more efficient processes.

The idea is to reduce the total material that goes into a product or its pack-aging without sacrificing quality or benefits to customers. Efforts to optimize material intensity lead companies to design and manufacture smaller or lighter products. Well-documented examples include using less metal in thinner bever-age cans, and using fewer materials in automobiles without reducing quality or safety. The WellMet2050 program at the University of Cambridge points out that most products could use one-third less metal without loss of performance.[2]

Enthusiasm for dematerialization has often focused on the use of digital technologies to provide information services without other media — e.g., "the paperless office" with online newspapers, electronic directories, and e-books. Their intended co-benefits are resource savings in material extraction; improved eco-design of products; and technological innovations in the organization and management of production processes. However, we must use a life-cycle lens to consider these changes to ensure that the required electronic equipment for digital music, for example, does not have a greater material burden than the replaced media.

Packaging optimization projects can often result in 100% ROI after the very first year. RG Barry's payback period for its packaging savings, described in Figure 5.3, was six months.

This resource-productivity model reduces the price of production, which increases competitiveness and lays the foundation for a higher bottom-line return. Business strategies built around radically increasing the productive use of natural resources can solve many environmental problems at a profit.

FIGURE 5.3

Examples of Dematerialization

Apple: Materials conservation was a key requirement in the design and manufacture of the Universal Motherboard Architecture (UMA) for Apple's Power Mac G4 Desktop Computer. Apple wanted to reduce materials because of the costs of the actual materials, warehousing, and associated labor for installing components. Material savings were made through substantial integration of parts and the use of larger chips. The dematerialized UMA used 50% fewer components than the previous Power Macintosh G3 logic board design and fewer than 1,000 components compared to over 2,000 for the G3. This resulted in time, resource, and cost savings by eliminating administrative and procurement efforts, logistics, and the actual installation of components onto the printed circuit board.

Source: A. Sweatman et al., "Design for Environment: A Case Study of the Power Mac G4 Desktop Computer," *Proceedings of the 2000 IEEE International Symposium on Electronics and the Environment,* IEEE Computer Society, Technical Committee on Electronics and the Environment, 2000, p. 13.

RG Barry: Slipper and footwear giant RG Barry reduced its shipping carton choices and saved more than $2.5 million in 18 months. The company replaced cartons made from five sheets of paper glued together with ones made from two sheets of paper surrounding a corrugated core. That format results in a stronger but thinner carton. The company also changed its standard box arrangement per carton from six wide by two deep to four by three. "Deeper is cheaper," since deeper cartons require less material for flaps than shallow ones. RG Barry also ensured that cartons used the entire pallet footprint, to save storage space. As a result of optimizing and dematerializing its shipping processes, the company spent 15% ($200,000) less on packaging, lowered inbound freight costs by 20% ($1.6 million), reduced the need for ocean containers, and trimmed storage expense by 25% ($1 million).

Source: Ken Mark, "How Reengineered Supply Chain Practices Revived Footwear Giant RG Barry" [accessed July 30, 2011], CTL.ca, April 20, 2011.

Bob Willard: In 2007 I dematerialized myself. I was doing about 75 talks a year and was appalled at my associated carbon footprint, mostly from airplane flights. Inspired by an audacious goal of reaching 10 times more sustainability champions without killing myself or the planet, I decided to clone myself. I made a DVD of my talk and began giving presentations using webinar and videoconference technology. I now give 80 to 100 talks a year, many virtually, plus thousands more through the DVD and its online counterpart. Dematerialization and substitution work, even when we take them personally.

Savings from Substitutions

Despite notions of market- or customer-driven corporate strategies, consumers do not choose the materials used in goods. Corporations do. Companies that wish to be sensitive to the environment consider what it takes to produce the raw materials they are purchasing. This "cradle-to-grave" perspective encourages them to look back to the cradle of the raw materials themselves — the energy and materials consumed in extracting, preparing, and transporting the purchased resources. There are a couple of ways to substitute less expensive, more environmentally friendly, more benign raw materials.

First, use materials with smaller "ecological rucksacks." Ecological rucksacks contain the total quantity of materials moved from nature to create products or services, including the hidden material flows that occur during the life cycle of the product. These rucksacks are a proxy for the environmental strain and resource inefficiency of the product or service.

Big rucksacks may equal higher prices, although "perverse subsidies" in many natural resource and fossil fuel industries distort this free market assumption. Such subsidies are "perverse" because they make citizens pay twice to encourage environmentally destructive behavior: their taxes pay for the subsidies, and then they pay the direct and indirect costs of environmental restoration and health care. By choosing raw materials that have smaller ecological rucksacks, companies will be in a better competitive position when subsidies are dropped. They will directly save money while indirectly contributing to the health of the planet.

Second, replace hazardous materials and chemicals with non-hazardous ones, as suggested by the two examples in Figure 5.4. As with dematerialization, this switch has a sometimes overlooked benefit in the form of labor savings from reduced handling costs due to use of less hazardous materials, and reduced staff time to monitor and report compliance with hazardous materials regulations.

Unfortunately, because of inequitable subsidies and short-term costing of traditional energy and materials, suggested substitutions often cost more today than their less benign alternatives. In some cases, the cost of recyclable materials exceeds the cost of raw materials. For example, virgin plastic resin costs 40% less than recycled resin.[3] We also need to consider the life-cycle energy requirements of substituted components to ensure we are not trading off a materials rucksack for an energy rucksack. Systems thinking is a must when evaluating alternatives.

FIGURE 5.4

Examples of Substitutions

Wood preservatives: For decades, wood was preserved with PCP (a fungicide) and lindane (an insecticide). Both preservatives were the focus of environmental protests in the 1970s and 1980s as a result of accidents during production and use; the persistence of the two chemicals in soil, food, and human tissues; and their contamination with ultra-toxic dioxins. They were classified as dangerous chemicals, and consumers rejected them for use in home projects. Producers in this market reacted to consumer demands for less-toxic products by replacing lindane with Pyrethroides and PCP with Dichlofluanid.

Rechargeable batteries: In the mid-1980s, the growing use of camcorders, household appliances, power tools, etc., fuelled an increased demand for smaller rechargeable batteries. At the time, nickel-cadmium batteries (NiCd) were favored, but due to their 15% cadmium content, these batteries are considered hazardous waste. When they were buried in landfills, cadmium leached into groundwater; when they were incinerated, cadmium was emitted into the atmosphere. In the 1990s, battery producers, mainly in Japan, anticipating a shortage of cadmium, developed nickel-metal–hydride (NiMH) and lithium ion (Li-ion) substitutes. NiMH cells have approximately twice the capacity of NiCd batteries. In many markets, such an improved technical performance, rather than environmental considerations, drove the introduction and acceptance of the new batteries.

Source: Joachim Lohse and Lothar Lißnar, "Substitution of Hazardous Chemicals in Products and Processes," Ökopol GmbH and Kooperationsstelle Hamburg, 2003, pp. 78–79 and 83.

Savings from Recycling and Reusing Onsite Waste

Reduce. Reuse. Recycle. The 3Rs of waste reduction lead to a materials-saving opportunity as companies source materials from what would otherwise be disposed of as waste. Many waste materials generated during the production process can be reused or recycled onsite in the plant or on the plant property, as shown in Figure 5.5. Executives are delighted when a firm does not waste materials and can make more products without buying more raw materials.

Some scrap material can be reused, either for its original purpose or in a new role, without requiring any major modification. Waste materials that are recycled, in contrast, may require significant physical, chemical, or biological processing to separate them from contaminants. There are several types of separation technology, described in Environment Canada's *Pollution Prevention Handbook:*

- To separate solid wastes, use such technologies as screening, magnetic separation, and air classification.
- To separate liquid wastes, use pH adjustment and precipitations, ion exchange, reverse osmosis, diffusion dialysis and electrodialysis, micro and ultra filtration, dewatering, extraction, and electrolytic methods.
- To separate gaseous wastes, adsorption, membranes, absorption, cryogenics, and condensation may be used.[4]

It is often necessary to separate toxic or hazardous wastes from recoverable materials, which adds to the challenge of recycling cost-effectively. Companies may have to resort to complex concentration technologies such as vacuum filtration, reverse osmosis, freeze vaporization, filter press, heat drying, and compaction. A break-even analysis will help you determine if these recovery efforts are more cost effective than purchasing virgin materials.

On the other hand, if the material can be recovered early in the production process, before it is contaminated with hazardous substances, the cost of separation can be avoided. At the point where the waste is first generated (e.g., where granular material has spilled from a feed hopper, or where flashing is trimmed from moulded products), it is still pure and can be reused as is.[5]

The further upstream in the production process the waste is recovered, the more likely it can be reused without resorting to exotic and expensive decontamination efforts. Also, the fewer toxic or hazardous substances used in processes, the less likelihood of contamination. Substitution facilitates recycling.

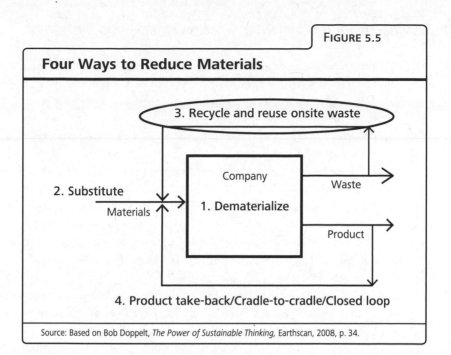

FIGURE 5.5

Four Ways to Reduce Materials

3. Recycle and reuse onsite waste

2. Substitute

Materials

Company

1. Dematerialize

Waste

Product

4. Product take-back/Cradle-to-cradle/Closed loop

Source: Based on Bob Doppelt, *The Power of Sustainable Thinking,* Earthscan, 2008, p. 34.

Savings from Product Take-Back / Closed-Loop Systems

The ultimate reduction of material occurs when companies take back their product at the end of its life (see examples in Figure 5.6). Customers enjoy the use of the product but do not own it. When they are finished with it, for whatever reason, the company takes back the materials, which it still owns, and uses them again. Rather than creating and selling products, the firm creates a service that provides the same benefit.

In business, the best way to make sure the company retains its asset after the consumer is finished using it is to lease it, the way people lease cars or computers. There is a subtle but profound difference in what consumers are purchasing. People are not buying a car; they are leasing personal transportation. They are not buying a computer; they are leasing computing capability. And as described in Figure 2.5, people using InterfaceFlor's Evergreen Lease have attractive floors without buying carpet.

Government "take back" regulations make this flow mandatory, but once a company understands the value of taking back its own products, it flips from fighting such regulations to insisting on them. Take-back, or extended producer responsibility (EPR), makes producers responsible for the environmental impacts of their products at the end of their products' useful life. As such, EPR shifts to private industry the responsibility for taking back, recycling, and ultimately disposing of any discarded material that would otherwise be managed by local governments. This incorporates the cost of product disposal or recycling into product price. Companies implement voluntary EPR initiatives when they are able to make a profit or gain a marketing advantage by taking back products, components, or extracted materials. In such cases, take-back is a proactive, financially attractive example of corporate social responsibility.

The real benefit of taking back "products of service" is the producer mindset it encourages. The company uses design for disassembly (DfD) so that it is easier to take the product apart to reuse its components. It uses different and fewer fasteners. It stamps plastic components with part numbers and other information instead of using gummy labels that require more labor and time to remove. It gets serious about using nontoxic materials in order to simplify handling processes.

Product take-back requires collaboration among manufacturers, retailers, users, and municipal governments. These players engage third-party recyclers to help with the logistics and recovery processes. A full cost analysis should be done to ensure the ongoing benefits of the closed-loop system outweigh the costs, but even a product as gigantic as a container ship can use cradle-to-cradle design, as explained in Figure 5.6.

FIGURE 5.6

Examples of Product Take-Back

Maersk: "Maersk Line will implement the most comprehensive cradle-to-cradle passport ever seen" for its new giant ships. They are completely recyclable. "The materials of the ships will all be marked and numbered — separating high and low grade steel, copper wiring, hazardous materials and waste ... The cradle to cradle passport will identify each and every nut and bolt of the giant 60,000 ton ships ... Based on the sorting it will be possible to reuse nearly all materials for new ships, making dangerous and polluting ship scrapping a thing of the past."

Source: "Maersk Line Triple-E: Total Vessel Recycling" [accessed July 30, 2011],
C2Cportal.net, April 5, 2011.

Sprint: In 2010, Sprint recycled 36% of all phones it sold. In 2011, the company announced a series of ambitious goals to reduce its e-waste streams, including a goal of collecting 100% of Sprint's own electronic waste for reuse and recycling by 2017, and collecting 90% of all phones sold for reuse or recycling by 2017.

Source: Matthew Wheeland, "Sprint Sets Ambitious Zero E-Waste Goal for 2017"
[accessed July 30, 2011], GreenBiz.com, May 26, 2011.

Nike: "Nike established a consumer-take-back program to recycle shoes, turning them into sport-courts ... Their executives publicly explain that if they were to continue to meet earnings and growth predicated on a business-as-usual industry standard model, they would literally require more natural resources than the earth has within our lifetimes."

Source: Brooke Farrell, "Debunking Six Myths about the Materials in Your Company's Dumpster"
[accessed July 30, 2011], EnvironmentalLeader.com, March 2011.

Savings on Water

Water is a very special material. Even if a business does not use a lot of water, it is likely to face some restrictions on its use, and an increase in its cost. If a business relies on water and operates in a drought-affected area, it is already acutely affected.

In industrial facilities, water is used in a wide range of activities.

- Incorporation in the final product
- Washing or rinsing of raw materials, intermediates, or final products
- Preparation of solvents or slurries
- Cleaning of equipment and space
- Removing or providing heat
- Meeting hygienic and domestic needs
- Irrigation of landscape space

Every good contains what is called "embodied water," which is a measure of the total amount of water used to produce that good or service. For example, it takes about 60 liters of water to make a typical ream of paper weighing 2.5 kilograms.

Water prices vary between cities or regions because of the range of water tariffs or sources of supply, but PepsiCo has found that even in places where water is inexpensive, the costs of treating it, using it, filtering it, and discharging it add up. In some cases, PepsiCo sees a tenfold increase in the fully measured cost of water between the time it enters a facility to the time a process is complete.[6] Fluke Corporation made a similar discovery, described in Figure 5.7.

Reducing the amount of water used in manufacturing can yield substantial savings. For example, sewage costs are usually based on the what-goes-in-must-come-out theory — they reflect the amount of water metered at the plant intake. If the company purchases less fresh water from the local utility, there is a corresponding reduction in sewage charges. Companies can reduce their need to purchase water by treating it themselves and reusing it in a closed-loop system.

A naturalized landscape that does not use pesticides and greatly reduces water consumption is a daily reminder to employees and passersby that the company cares. About 40% to 80% of a water utility's peak demand in the summer is driven by landscape watering, which can be reduced by about 50% by relatively modest improvements: using water-frugal grasses, growing flora indigenous to the region, and converting lawns into diverse native grasslands, bushes, and trees.

FIGURE 5.7

Examples of Water Savings

Fluke: Fluke Corporation in Seattle, which manufactures industrial testing equipment, found it paid for water four times: when it purchased the water in the first place, when it treated the water to production standards, when it treated the water prior to discharge, and when it paid its sewage fees. Over two years, Fluke reduced water use from 2.5 million gallons per month to 400,000 gallons per month, resulting in bottom line savings of $138,000 per year.

Source: Scott D. Johnson, "Identification and Selection of Environmental Performance Indicators: Application of the Balanced Scorecard Approach," *Corporate Environmental Strategy* 5, no. 4, Summer 1998, p. 40.

Lockheed Martin: In 2008, Lockheed Martin set goals of reducing water use by 25% by the end of 2012, based on 2007 levels. The targets are absolute reductions, not reductions in intensity (in which consumption, waste, and emissions are measured in comparison to other factors, such as revenue, units of production, or number of employees). By the end of 2010 the company had implemented efficiency and conservation measures that cut water use by 22%. In the first quarter of 2011, the firm surpassed its goals by bringing the reduction in water consumption to 27%.

Source: Leslie Guevarra, "Lockheed Saves $2.6M in IT Energy Costs; Tops Water, Waste Targets" [accessed July 30, 2011], GreenBiz.com, April 20, 2011.

Savings on Consumables and Paper

Every employee is a resource gatekeeper. Suppose a company educated its employees to be more aware consumers, and they started to look for more enviro-friendly actions in their homes and workplaces. There is evidence that employees become more careful about consumables at work if they are trained to be more frugal without sacrificing quality. The forestry company Weyerhaeuser, for example, participated in a program, based on Vicki Robin's book *Your Money Or Your Life,* that taught employees better money management and more conscious spending practices. In a follow-up survey of employees a year after they had taken the workshop, 28% said they were more frugal with company resources than before.[7]

"While many organizations focus on big-picture environmental opportunities, such as reducing greenhouse gas emissions and increasing renewable energy investments, sometimes the most elemental facets of business get overlooked," according to Ralph Reid, VP of Corporate Social Responsibility at Sprint. "One of the most basic materials in business is paper, used in everything from billing to photocopying, marketing, and reporting. According to US Environmental Protection Agency data, the average US office worker uses 10,000 sheets of copy paper each year, which contributes to an annual consumption of about 85 million tons of paper and paperboard. According to ForestEthics, a member of the Environmental Paper Network, the number of pages of paper consumed in US offices is growing by about 20% each year. Meeting the demands of this great paper chase within today's corporations requires a resource-intensive manufacturing process that is dependent on forests, water and energy."[8]

As shown in Figure 5.8, paper and cardboard constitute over half the waste from a typical office. Paper waste can be avoided in two ways. First, use less by converting to electronic documents, invoices, bills, and copies. Reducing paper usage avoids forest depletion and shrinks the company's environmental footprint. It also helps the bottom line. Second, sort the paper waste so that it can be sold to recyclers instead of thrown into a landfill. This helps convert an expense into a revenue stream, further helping the bottom line.

As with energy savings, avoiding paper waste depends on employee cooperation and engagement. Without that cooperation, policies and proclamations are futile. With it, companies can save tons of unwanted or unneeded paper and paper waste.

FIGURE 5.8

Typical Waste Stream

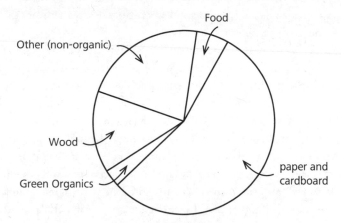

In 2006–7, Australia generated 14.4 million tonnes
of commercial and industrial waste.
Of this, **44.5% was dumped in landfill** and
55.5% was recycled.

Source: Adapted from Jon Dee, *Small Business Big Opportunity,* Sensis Pty Ltd, 2010, p. 62. The book is available as a free download at about.sensis.com.au/small-business/free-sustainable-growth-book/.

Potential Materials Savings Help Build a Sustainability Capital Reserve

Figures 5.9 and 5.10 show the calculations for the savings in material and water expenses for Sam's Solutions and M&D Corp. As usual, the methodology is the same for both generic companies.

The cost of materials and water today is as shown on the companies' data sheets (Figures 1.25 and 1.26). The amount of material and water used for useful product is 70%, consistent with the assumption in the previous chapter that 30% ends up as waste. We are only looking at saving the 70%, since savings related to the other 30% are addressed in the waste reduction calculations.

We treat the potential for reducing material much the same way we treated the potential for reducing waste — very conservatively. We assume that dematerialization, substitution, reuse, and product take-back efforts reduce the overall cost of materials and water by only 10%. We anticipate that some dematerialization savings will be offset by higher costs for substitute greener materials; some savings from reusing onsite waste are offset by the cost of separation and recovery; and some savings from recapturing materials from returned products are offset by the cost of closed-loop logistical systems required for product take-back. Even so, this benefit is one of the highest contributors to the bottom line.

There is an understandable temptation to simply pool these savings with savings from other benefit areas and account for them in general accounts that flow through to the bottom line. Instead, we propose that half the savings be set aside in a rotating pool of capital to fund other sustainability projects. We treat this Sustainability Capital Reserve as free cash flow that can be reinvested in sustainability capital projects without competing with other projects for the company's limited capital funds. This provides an opportunity for special hurdle rates and payback periods for sustainability projects. Using some of the savings on material to reinvest in company efficiencies and research on break-through sustainability innovations enables the benefit to be compounded as these investment seeds are later harvested. Similarly, we contribute half the savings in waste to the Sustainability Capital Reserve, and there is no reason why some of the savings from other benefit areas could not be added as well. We are simply illustrating the principle of this approach using waste and materials savings.

If we set aside half the savings on materials and water for the Sustainability Capital Reserve, the remaining half is a benefit that flows through to the bottom line, as shown in Figures 5.9 and 5.10 for Sam's Solutions and M&D Corp.

FIGURE 5.9

Sam's Solutions' Potential Reduced Materials and Water Expenses

Cost of materials and water today	**$50,000**
Assumption: Percentage of materials and water used in products rather than being wasted	*70%*
Cost of materials and water used for products sold/not wasted	**$35,000**
Assumption: Percentage savings in materials and water from further dematerialization, substitutions, product take-back, and reusing previously wasted materials and water	*10%*
Savings in materials and water expenses	**$3,500**
Assumption: Percentage of materials savings set aside in the Sustainability Capital Reserve for investments in sustainability projects	*50%*
Contribution to Sustainability Capital Reserve	**$1,750**
Reduced materials and water expenses in 3 to 5 years	**$1,750**

FIGURE 5.10

M&D Corp.'s Potential Reduced Materials and Water Expenses

Cost of materials and water today	**$150,000,000**
Assumption: Percentage of materials and water used in products, rather than being wasted	*70%*
Cost of materials and water used for products sold/not wasted	**$105,000,000**
Assumption: Percentage savings in materials and water from further dematerialization, substitutions, product take-back, and reusing previously wasted materials and water	*10%*
Savings in materials and water expenses	**$10,500,000**
Assumption: Percentage of materials savings set aside in the Sustainability Capital Reserve for investments in sustainability projects	*50%*
Contribution to Sustainability Capital Reserve	**$5,250,000**
Reduced materials and water expenses in 3 to 5 years	**$5,250,000**

Increased Employee Productivity

Engagement represents, perhaps, the most touchy-feely and fuzzy word in the lexicon of management, so let us offer a brief definition of it. An "engaged employee" is one who "is fully involved in, and enthusiastic about, his or her work, and thus will act in a way that furthers their organization's interests"... Now, if employee engagement is so important when it comes to company performance, how can we get more of it? Interestingly enough, embedding social and environmental considerations into the company's purpose, strategy, and operations might just be the best way to go.

— Chris Lazlo and Nadia Zhexembayeva, *Embedded Sustainability*

Purpose Powers Performance

According to Nicholas Imparato and Oren Harari in *Jumping the Curve*, current wisdom on employee performance is summarized in the following formula:

> **Performance = Ability x Motivation[1]**

As Daniel Pink reminds us in *Drive*, extrinsic carrot-and-stick motivators work fine for simple mechanical tasks. However, if we want conceptual, innovative thinking, we need intrinsic motivators. Pink says intrinsic motivators have three elements: Autonomy — the desire to direct our own lives; Mastery — the urge to get better and better at *something that matters;* and Purpose — the yearning to do what we do in the service of something larger than ourselves.[2] Sustainability strategies and programs provide purpose and an opportunity to do something that matters. They inspire feelings of pride and of satisfaction that we are making a contribution to society.

The team-consulting company Belgard-Fisher-Rayner created an engagement model (see Figure 6.1) that shows how four factors combine to yield employee desire to strive above and beyond their defined role. Employees are committed to a project or overarching goal when they understand what it is (Clarity); see how it benefits the company (Relevance); have a personal opportunity to shape and implement the initiative (Involvement); and find that it resonates with their personal values as a worthwhile goal (*Meaning*). Meaning is the energy source for the commitment. Through our work we seek a sense of purpose, contribution, value, and hope. When we achieve fulfillment at work, we become fully engaged and innovate beyond our wildest dreams.

Visions related to sustainable development contain economic, social, and environmental dimensions — it would be difficult to find a more powerfully inspiring trio of aspirations. A company taking on an ambitious sustainability mission creates an energized, committed, and motivated workforce that is more productive and innovative. Zero emissions, self-sufficient energy production, zero waste, and restoration of the social and environmental health of the planet are powerful vision elements for a company. They are "Big Hairy Audacious Goals" (BHAGs), as Collins and Porras would say,[3] and they provide the purpose and meaning that intrinsically fuel productivity and innovation.

As Thomas Edison said, "Vision without execution is hallucination." So is vision without money. The business case finds the money to execute the vision.

FIGURE 6.1

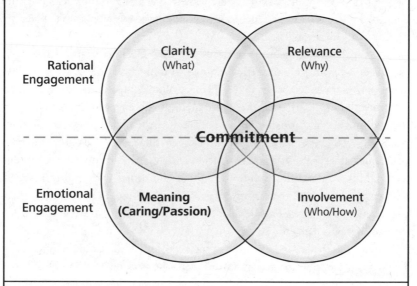

Four Commitment/Engagement Factors

Rational Engagement

Clarity (What)

Relevance (Why)

Commitment

Emotional Engagement

Meaning (Caring/Passion)

Involvement (Who/How)

Source: Belgard-Fisher-Rayner Inc. © 1991. Used with permission. This model was used extensively in leadership development at IBM Canada in the 1990s.

Engagement Drives Business Results

The reason companies want engaged employees is that they want better business results. Happy employees are a convenient by-product. As shown in Figure 6.2, there is clear evidence that high employee engagement is related to improved organizational results.

A Gallup Consulting study of data from over 152 organizations contrasts the upside of having an engaged workforce with the downside of having a disengaged workforce. As shown in Figure 6.3, Gallup compared the performance of companies in the top quartile of companies with engaged employees with the performance of companies in the bottom quartile with disengaged employees. There was a dramatic difference between the top and bottom quartile companies' track records in safety incidents, employee turnover, and absenteeism. More importantly, Gallup found that companies with highly engaged workgroups have 18% greater productivity and 12% higher profitability than organizations with lower engagement in their same industry, as well as 2.6 times the earnings-per-share growth rate.

Companies that connect people to their passions and enable them to make a significant contribution to causes they care about as human beings will see a direct correlation to higher levels of engagement and significant business benefits. According to a WorkUSA survey, companies with engaged employees experience 26% higher revenue per employee, 13% higher total returns to shareholders, and a 50% higher market premium.[4]

Do companies want lower absenteeism, lower employee turnover, and fewer safety incidents? Yes. Do they want higher customer satisfaction, higher employee productivity, greater profitability, and faster growth? You bet. These benefits come from more engaged employees, and sustainability efforts contribute to that higher level of engagement. CEOs who want to improve their companies' hard business results would be well advised to focus more on soft, meaningful, impactful sustainability efforts.

Before we explore sustainability-related contributors to employee productivity and innovation, we set the stage by elaborating on how:

- Engagement enables productivity and innovation
- Sustainability programs promote productivity and innovation
- Volunteerism vaults employee engagement and productivity

FIGURE 6.2

Engagement Helps Business Results

- Companies with engaged employees **grew profits three times faster** than competitors.

- Highly engaged organizations have **87% less staff turnover** and **20% better performance** than average.

- **Operating income** of companies with engaged employees **improved by 19% in one year** vs. a decline of 33% for companies with low levels of employee engagement.

- **59%** of engaged employees say their job brings out their most **creative ideas** vs. 3% of disengaged employees.

Source: "Engage: Inspiring Employees about Sustainability," World Business Council for Sustainable Development, August 2010, p. 6.

FIGURE 6.3

Engagement Drives Business Results

Difference between the top quartile of companies with actively engaged employees and the bottom quartile of companies with disengaged employees

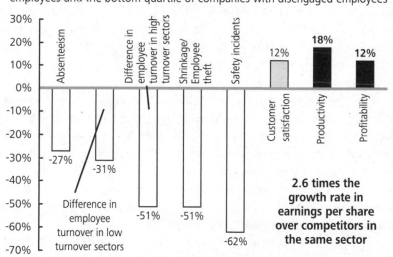

Source: Adapted from "Employee Engagement: What's Your Engagement Ratio?" Gallup Consulting, 2008, p. 3. Based on Gallup Consulting's analysis of 125 organizations.

Engagement Enables Productivity and Innovation

If we are to assess the connections between purpose and employee engagement, between employees' engagement and productivity, and between innovation and business results, we need to know how we would recognize an engaged employee if we saw one.

Hewitt Associates provides a helpful definition of engagement, as shown in Figure 6.4: "Capturing the hearts and minds of employees." This is the holy grail of managers and human resources professionals. The "Say" behavior helps to attract top talent to the organization through word of mouth; the "Stay" behavior mitigates attrition of top talent who are already working in the company. (We discuss these two in more detail in the next chapter on hiring and attrition.) The "Strive" behavior drives productivity and innovation as employees "strive to achieve above and beyond what is expected in their daily lives." It is the "Strive" behavior that interests us in this chapter, since it connects with motivation, engagement, productivity, and innovation.

A survey by Greenomics in 2010 confirmed that 97% of executives believe innovation is important to becoming sustainable.[5] It is essential in creating future value for the firm. When innovation is mentioned, many of us equate it with technological breakthroughs. It is softer than that.

Organizations do not innovate; inspired people innovate, at all levels in the organization. A high-performance culture unleashes the creativity of people who are intellectually and emotionally committed to clear, relevant, and meaningful work that they helped shape. Whether the goal is to deliver greater value through innovative new products and services or to reinvent an entire business model, engaged and committed employees figure out the best answers faster and more efficiently than external experts. All we need to do is provide a culture within which human ingenuity can flourish.

We are intrinsically energized by challenges. During studies for my master's degree, a professor advised me to forget about trying to justify sustainability strategies in the for-profit sector. I set out to prove him wrong, leading to my master's thesis, my first book, and this revised edition. We innovate because we want to make a difference, not because we are told to. We enjoy mulling over solutions while commuting, showering, or even dreaming. Sustainability challenges "awaken, nurture and develop the primal need that all people have to create something extraordinary."[6] They're also fun.

Innovation and productivity are increasingly paired. By elevating engagement, we raise both. It's a two-for-one deal.

FIGURE 6.4

Employee Engagement Defined

Engagement is the state of emotional and intellectual commitment to an organization — the degree to which you have captured the hearts and minds of your employees.

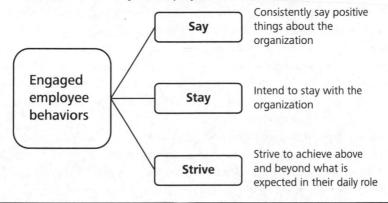

Engaged employee behaviors

Say — Consistently say positive things about the organization

Stay — Intend to stay with the organization

Strive — Strive to achieve above and beyond what is expected in their daily role

Source: Adapted from "Engaging Employees through CSR," Canadian Business for Social Responsibility (CBSR) and Hewitt Associates webinar, January 2010. Based on a slide used during the webinar.

CSR Programs Promote Productivity and Engagement

In 2010, Hewitt Associates, the global human resources consulting company, partnered with Canadian Business for Social Responsibility (CBSR) to understand the relationship between employees' perceptions of their companies' corporate social responsibility (CSR) efforts, their level of engagement, and other work–environment factors. Hewitt and CBSR gathered opinions from over 100,000 employees and 2,000 leaders from more than 230 workplaces. A good CSR reputation is one of 21 factors that Hewitt has identified which correlate positively with employee engagement. The straight-line correlation (see Figure 6.5) shows that the more employees agree that their company is proactively pursuing worthy environmental and social activities, the more they are engaged. It is hard to prove a cause-and-effect relationship but, at a minimum, it is a happy correlation.

Hewitt's research found that CSR programs encompass the seven dimensions shown in Figure 6.6. In a sustainable enterprise, every employee is engaged, and sustainability efforts are measured, rewarded, and aligned throughout the firm, a reality addressed by the corporate governance and employee relations dimensions. Equally important is the company's relationship with its customers and suppliers, including human rights issues within the firm. Programs that address the company's impacts on the environment and on the community provide opportunities for employee volunteerism (which we cover next).

Hewitt's seven dimensions provide a wonderfully holistic template for corporate CSR programs. They show that there is no magic silver bullet. A company needs to be strong in all seven areas to be deemed a good corporate citizen by its own employees.

Gallup has done extensive surveys and identified 12 factors that drive employee engagement.[7] Most of the factors are about the job itself, such as opportunities to do what the employee does best every day and access to tools required to do the job well. Another factor is relationships at work — for example, being recognized in the last week by the managers. Only one of the 12 could be seen as relating directly to CSR: "The mission of this organization makes me feel my job is important."

Gallup's research, like Hewitt's, suggests that CSR is only one of many factors that drive engagement. However, it is gaining in importance, in concert with society's concern about sustainability issues and the role of corporations in helping to address them.

FIGURE 6.5

Engagement Correlates with CSR

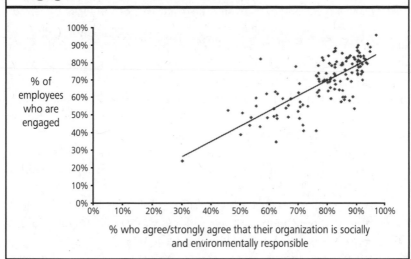

% of employees who are engaged

% who agree/strongly agree that their organization is socially and environmentally responsible

Source: Adapted from "Engaging Employees through CSR," CBSR and Hewitt Associates webinar, January 2010. Based on a slide used during the webinar.

FIGURE 6.6

Seven Dimensions of Company CSR Efforts

This is a socially and environmentally responsible organization

Community and Society

This organization plays an active role in the community

Customer Relationships

This organization is fair, respectful, and honest with customers/clients

Environment

This organization works to minimize the impact of its operations, products/ services on the environment

Supplier Relations

This organization makes purchasing decisions that take social and environ- mental values into consideration

Corporate Governance

This organization considers long-term social, environmental, and economic impacts when it makes decisions

Employee Relations

Employees are treated fairly, respectfully, and honestly in this organization

Human Rights

This organization respectfully manages human rights in its operations

Source: Adapted from "Engaging Employees through CSR," CBSR and Hewitt Associates webinar, January 2010. Based on a slide used during the webinar.

Volunteerism Vaults Employee Engagement and Productivity

Employee volunteer programs are an important part of the social dimension of a company's sustainability efforts. A surprise co-benefit when the company allows employees to give their talent, time, and energy to causes that they personally care about, and which align with the company's mission, is the volunteers' higher level of engagement and productivity back in the workplace. Two-thirds of workers surveyed in the UK said that having paid time off during working hours to commit to charity work would "significantly improve" motivation.[8] In Ireland, a recent study found that 87% of employees who volunteered with their companies reported an improved perception of their employer. More importantly, a whopping 82% felt more committed to the organization they worked for.[9]

The cause could be Habitat for Humanity, helping the homeless, tutoring disadvantaged school children, a neighborhood cleanup campaign, helping a village abroad — anything worthy that allows employees to volunteer to help. Employees' engagement is fuelled by their caring for the program's outcomes; people find personal meaning when making a difference.

As shown in Figure 6.7, volunteers also feel fulfilled and energized when they see they are making a difference, and that energy transfers back into the work environment. In *Corporate Karma*, Peggie Pelosi tells about her experience at USANA, summarized in Figure 6.8: same employees, same customers, and same products — double the sales after the volunteer program was implemented. Pelosi cautions that the recipe for success is important. When establishing a volunteer program, the cause must be carefully chosen. The company should ensure the purpose of the non-profit organization it allies with meshes with the firm's values and mission. The CEO, the board, even customers should participate, to reinforce its importance. Such an alliance needs to be a strategic initiative, more profound and enduring than a one-time intervention like helping the food bank at Christmas. Progress should be tracked and reported against declared meaningful goals to emphasize that this is a serious company focus.

In addition to increasing productivity, volunteer programs also develop employees' leadership capability, build new transferable skills, enhance loyalty and retention, stimulate innovation, engender trust in leadership, build a sense of camaraderie with interdepartmental colleagues, improve the business's community relationship, and reduce absenteeism.[10] When the whole company becomes inspired by giving back, volunteer programs create employee engagement and improved business results.

FIGURE 6.7

Volunteerism Increases Satisfaction

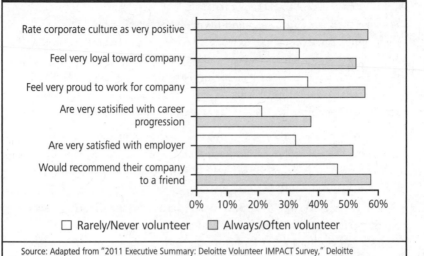

Rate corporate culture as very positive

Feel very loyal toward company

Feel very proud to work for company

Are very satisified with career progression

Are very satisfied with employer

Would recommend their company to a friend

0%   10%   20%   30%   40%   50%   60%

☐ Rarely/Never volunteer   ☐ Always/Often volunteer

Source: Adapted from "2011 Executive Summary: Deloitte Volunteer IMPACT Survey," Deloitte Development LLC, 2011, p. 1. Based on a survey of millennials or "Generation Y," born after 1977.

FIGURE 6.8

USANA: Volunteerism → Engagement

USANA had flat sales for several years.

Peggie Pelosi was appointed VP Sales in 2000.

To energize the workforce and transform corporate culture, she partnered with Children's Hunger Fund (CHF) to provide nutritional supplements to children in the developing world. She engaged all employees, customers, board members, and shareholders, donating company products, money, and **volunteer time.**

The Result?

- More than **doubled sales** (from $120M to $270M) in three years
- **Stock value rose 3,000%** (from $1.70 to $70.00)
- Increased donations to CHF (from $120K to over $1M)

Source: Adapted from Peggie Pelosi, *Corporate Karma*, Orenda Publishing, 2007, pp. 6–7

Increased Productivity from Reduced Absenteeism

Unplanned absenteeism costs much more than most companies realize and is often not well tracked or managed. The facts and figures in Figure 6.9 show that there are large direct and indirect costs of high rates of absenteeism. When employees do not come to work, co-workers experience lost productivity, and there are costs associated with finding and paying for temporary replacements. We conservatively assume absenteeism costs 2% of payroll today.

Studies suggest 60% to 70% of employee absenteeism is due to reasons other than illness. The following are common reasons employees tend to miss work:

- Employees are stressed or preoccupied by personal matters, such as parental concerns, marital problems, community involvement, family well-being, care for elderly relatives, care for severely ill immediate family members, and so on.
- Employees are overwhelmed with their current working situation, or they are overworked due to workforce reductions and voluntary turnover.
- Employees are dissatisfied with their current working conditions, position, team performance, supervisor, or overall organization.
- Employees are not committed to their team, department, or organization.
- Employees are not challenged by their position and have increased feelings of burnout.[11]

Employers can influence the approximately 60% of employee absenteeism, and the resulting loss of productivity, that results from personal matters by giving employees flexible work schedules and work-at-home options. These approaches help employees juggle stressful demands on the home front with workplace requirements. An employer can also directly influence the other main causes of absenteeism in the list by taking steps to improve employees' intrinsic motivation. For example, an employer might ensure production goals are realistic, increase desirable job responsibilities, and improve working conditions.

Governance policies that treat employees with respect and care make a difference to absenteeism rates, as do sustainability-related personnel policies. As just discussed, employees who volunteer through their workplace report improved physical and emotional health, as well as more positive attitudes toward their colleagues and company. We assume sustainability-related human resources policies and programs could create a high-performing company culture that will reduce absenteeism by 20%.

FIGURE 6.9

Canadian Absenteeism Statistics

- Canadian organizations report an annual absenteeism rate of 6.6 days lost per full-time employee, which costs organizations an average of 2.6% of payroll.
- Employees with weak employment relations miss an average of 5.9 days due to illness compared to 3.7 days per year for those with strong relationships.
- The estimated cost of absenteeism due to staff experiencing family to work interference is approximately $450 million/year.
- $33 billion is lost in productivity annually due to mental illness in Canada. Depression and anxiety alone cost the economy $14.4 billion per year.
- 50% of Canadians have high levels of stress caused by an unhealthy work environment where job demands exceed control; excessive workloads are the norm; decision making is top down; and managerial support for work-life balance is lacking.
- Caring for children with asthma is the third-leading cause of lost work time for adults in Canada. One in five children in Canada has asthma.
- Health absenteeism directly and indirectly costs businesses about 9% of payroll. This is the total direct cost of providing incidental absence benefits of 2%, plus replacement labor and loss of productivity of 4%, plus direct costs of short term disability and long-term disability of 1%, plus 2% of indirect associated costs.

Source: "What Studies Are Telling Us" [accessed July 30, 2011], LewisDaly.com, 2010.

Increased Productivity from
More Telecommuting and Less Travel

Exploiting the potential of e-business, e-mail, and secure intranets can significantly reduce the environmental impact of doing business. Telecommunications eliminate the need for many office workers to commute every day. Working from home offers benefits for the environment, the company, and employees.

The environment benefits from a reduction in vehicular emissions, less pavement, and more green spaces.

The company benefits through financial savings. Figure 6.10 shows that 40% of employees have jobs that are compatible with telecommuting and outlines the financial benefits if just 100 employees work from home half the time. We conservatively assume 10% of employees could telecommute.

Employees benefit by eliminating the time, expense, and hassle of commuting. They may also experience a more enjoyable and relaxed working environment. Surveys show that 30% of employees would take a pay cut in order to telecommute and enjoy an improved, more discretionary balance between their work and personal lives. Employees who work half of their time out of the office save about two workweeks of commuting time and anywhere from $2,000 to $6,800 because they are using less gas and reducing parking, food, clothing, and other expenses.[12] The needs of disabled workers are also often better addressed through telecommuting.

The icing on the cake is the potential for increased employee productivity. IBM Canada has seen teleworker productivity improvements of up to 50%.[13] We conservatively assume a 10% productivity improvement.

Reducing business travel to meet with clients or colleagues, or to attend conferences, and replacing it with teleconferencing and videoconferencing, also frees up more productive time during the workday. For most businesses, teleconferencing via the phone is already here. Videoconferencing, which uses digital video cameras connected to home and office personal computers, is widely available and effective, with potentially huge travel and pollution savings. A Carbon Disclosure Project study calculated that businesses in the United States and the United Kingdom could save $19 billion on travel costs between 2010 and 2020 by deploying 10,000 videoconference/telepresence units. A co-benefit is a saving of 5.5 metric tons of carbon.[14]

We assume an additional 10% of personnel could reduce their business travel, and their productivity would be boosted by a modest 5% by doing so. The savings on travel costs are a bonus that should be added into the business case, if they can be estimated and are significant enough.

FIGURE 6.10

Telecommuting Savings

At least 40% of employees have jobs that are compatible with telecommuting, but less than 2% of employees work from home the majority of their time. If the 80% of workers who want to telecommute did so — even if it was only half of the time — businesses could save $124 billion in real estate, electricity, and related costs; they could also increase productivity by more than $235 billion. Letting one employee work half of their time out of the office saves their company about $10,000 per year. Businesses that let 100 employees work half of their time from home can save about $1.1 million a year.

- $576,000 would come from increased productivity as employees experienced fewer interruptions, practiced better time management, and put in more hours by working when they would have been commuting.
- $304,000 would come from savings in electricity, real estate, parking lot leases, furniture, supplies, maintenance, and space consolidation.
- $113,000 would come from fewer unscheduled absences and less sick time, and from employees working while sick or waiting for personal appointments (cable installation, parcel delivery, etc.) that would normally result in a full day off work.
- $76,000 would be saved due to lower employee turnover.

Source: Kate Lister and Tom Hamish, "Workshifting Benefits: The Bottom Line," TeleworkResearchNetwork.com (TRN), May 2010, available at www.workshifting.com. The benefits are based on TRN's telework savings calculator, which assumes 50, 100, or 500 employees are teleworking half the time, as well as the total savings for the United States.

Increased Productivity from Green Buildings

Green buildings provide surprising increases in employee productivity. Paul Hawken, Amory Lovins, and Hunter Lovins, authors of *Natural Capitalism*, quantify productivity gains of 6% to 16% from people working in well-designed, energy-efficient buildings.[15] The Green Building Council of Australia estimates that occupants are 1% to 25% more productive in green buildings.[16] Joseph Romm, author of *Cool Companies*, calculates that productivity benefits due to workplace green design range from 7% to 15%. In addition, Romm notes a drop in sick leave and absenteeism.[17] Since a typical office pays about 100 times as much for people as it does for energy, this increased productivity in people is worth 6 to 16 times as much as eliminating the entire energy bill.[18]

Figure 6.11 shows how this productivity gain should be factored into the business case for green buildings. Gregory Kats at MIT found that four of the attributes associated with green buildings — increased ventilation control, increased temperature control, increased lighting control, and increased daylighting — positively and significantly correlate with increased productivity. Increases in tenant control over ventilation, temperature, and lighting each provide measured benefits ranging from 0.5% to 34%.[19]

Mail sorters at the main US Post Office in Reno, NV, became the most productive and error-free in the western United States after a green energy and lighting upgrade in their building. The $300,000 upgrade produced $50,000 in yearly energy and maintenance savings and a whopping $400,000 annual productivity gain from employees.[20] After VeriFone renovated its building, beating California's strict Title 24 building code by 60%, employees were 5% more productive, and absenteeism dropped by 45%. These benefits reduced the payback period from 7.5 years to less than a year, for a return on investment of more than 100%.[21]

Given the 0.5% to 34% range of estimates of increased productivity for employees working in green buildings, we conservatively assume a 10% gain. Some employees may already be working in such facilities; some may never be able to. We very conservatively assume another 10% of the workplace can be greened within the next five years, so the resulting productivity gain is the product of those two percentages: 1%. We further conservatively assume only 10% of this 1% productivity gain is in addition to gains already counted, as explained later.

FIGURE 6.11

Green Building Business Case

Financial Benefits of Green Buildings
Summary of Findings (per ft²)

Category	20-Year Net Present Value
Energy Savings	$5.80
Emissions Savings	$1.20
Water Savings	$0.50
Operations and Maintenance Savings	$8.50
Productivity and Health Benefits	$36.90 to $55.30
Subtotal	**$52.90 to $71.30**
Average Extra Cost of Building Green	**(-3.00 to -$5.00)**
Total 20-Year Net Benefit	**$50 to $60**

Source. Gregory H. Kats, "Green Building Costs and Financial Benefits," Massachusetts Technology Collaborative, 2003, p. 8. Data from Capital E Analysis.

Increased Productivity and Innovation from Improved Collaboration

The whole is greater than the sum of its parts: success in the new economy is dependent on creative collaborative relationships. Successful companies collaborate with a broader network of interdepartmental colleagues and external stakeholders to invent breakthrough ideas so they can thrive in today's more complex economy.

In many large organizations, working relationships between departments verge on dysfunctional. Misaligned goals cause internal rivalry between organizational silos, wasting attention and energy that should be used to challenge the company's external competitors. The more opportunities interdepartmental staff have to get to know each other and work together on common purposes, the better they develop interdepartmental esprit de corps. Training programs, like the one outlined in Figure 6.12 for Marks and Spencer, help overcome interdepartmental friction as employees work together to accomplish worthy sustainability-related objectives. These cohesion-building opportunities have a beneficial spillover effect: departments continue to collaborate outside sustainability projects and innovate together to transform the firm's products, services, processes, and culture.

Wiki-savvy employees can tap in to more possibilities of peer- and cyber-space-connected collaboration,[22] sharing fresh and radical thinking through platforms that enable self-organized mass teamwork among internal and external stakeholders. The networked world provides new ways of navigating the white waters of change and complexity for the benefit of all. Employees find it is fulfilling to innovate and collaborate their way through the necessary transformation.

When sustainability is at the core of business and is connected to the conscience of an organization, it can be a platform for greater business growth and innovation, and an essential pillar of creative business partnerships. Now more than ever, strategic partnerships between industry and governments, academia, and non-government organizations (NGOs) are critical to finding solutions to challenges such as supply chain footprints, access to clean water, and harnessing renewable energy sources. The seeds of multi-stakeholder collaboration blossom in wonderfully innovative solutions to business challenges, with exciting co-benefits for our collective sustainability challenges.

The resulting productivity gain from improved company-wide collaboration would be significant. To be conservative, we assume it adds another 10% to the productivity of 10% of the employees, and that only 10% of this gain has not already been counted elsewhere, as explained next.

FIGURE 6.12

Employee Engagement at Marks and Spencer

Marks and Spencer (M&S), the United Kingdom's largest clothing retailer, which "has stated publicly that sustainability is critical to future business success," took top prize in the 2011 Guardian Sustainable Business Engaging Employees contest with its Plan A initiative. Plan A ("there is no Plan B") is designed to make M&S the world's most sustainable retailer. The company claims it is "the most successful motivational and change management programme ever delivered within M&S, enabling people from different parts of the business and functions to work together for a common goal."

By early 2011, Plan A had improved energy efficiency in stores by 19% and fuel efficiency for clothing deliveries by 30%. Carbon emissions were down by 20% per square foot. M&S had raised levels of sustainably sourced wood and fish to 72% and 62%, respectively.

The panel of judges for the Guardian award described the plan as "a solid mix of inspiration, incentives and measurement" that would be embedded deeply into the M&S culture. For example, a proportion of director bonuses is based on their Plan A achievements and leadership, and "employee engagement" is one of 180 measurable sustainability commitments the company wants to achieve by 2015. Each of M&S's 690 UK stores has a Plan A champion, a volunteer who encourages colleagues to cut electricity consumption, reduce paper use, and recover more waste. Stores are ranked each month to foster a sense of competition. On team days, champions meet to share ideas.

The company also seeks to engage its 76,000 staff at home by offering discounted solar technology, bikes, train fares, and eco-holidays. Employees could also claim a free energy monitor worth $50 and free attic insulation worth $400. Every employee can take one day a year, with pay, to work for a charity, and the company recognizes outstanding volunteer work.

New recruits often cite Plan A as the reason they're applying for work at the company, and store-level Plan A champions are increasingly moving into the company's management development program, allowing M&S to retain good, motivated talent.

In addition to enhancing employee engagement and interdepartmental relationships, Plan A generated $82 million additional profit in 2009–10, which M&S invested back into the business.

Source: Jackie Wills, "M&S — Wholly Embracing Staff in Plan To Become the World's Most Sustainable Retailer" [accessed July 30, 2011], Guardian.co.uk, May 26, 2011, www.guardian.co.uk/sustainable-business/staff-plan-worlds-sustainable-retailer.

Increased Productivity and Innovation from Higher Engagement

Productivity improves when a company gets more and better results from the same workforce. Productivity also improves with innovation, as employees or others come up with more efficient ways to do the same work.

As discussed earlier, engaged employees are more productive and more innovative. This is good for business. When the current cohort of employees generates more output, the company avoids the cost of adding additional employees to the payroll in order to reap the same benefits. It also avoids the cost of hiring consultants to help find and capture the benefits. Less absenteeism, more telecommuting, and less business travel provide direct sustainability-related productivity benefits by allowing more time on the job and eliminating the need to hire more people to fill in for the lost time.

In Figures 6.13 and 6.14, these three contributors, along with green buildings, collaboration, and engagement, are sized for Sam's Solutions and M&D Corp. as a percentage of the current workforce payroll that the company would need to add in order to generate equivalent productivity benefits.

Although we could reasonably assume that, after five years, 50% to 75% of the workforce will be engaged and their innovative ideas will enable them to be 10% to 25% more productive, we very conservatively assume only 25% of the employees are engaged, and they are just 10% more productive as a result.

As explained earlier, sustainability strategies result in green buildings, improved collaboration, and higher levels of engagement. These stimulate productivity and innovation benefits. However, we conservatively claim only 10% of each of these three benefits because we assume the value of 90% of these innovative ideas is already accounted for in other sustainability benefits — i.e., increased revenue, reduced energy expenses, reduced materials expenses, and reduced waste expenses. That is, the current workforce employees figured out how to do more with less. We avoid double-counting by not claiming these sustainability-related benefits again within our productivity category. So we use a very conservative 10% fraction of the added payroll cost of new employees who would otherwise have to be hired to generate the equivalent productivity benefits.

We are not advocating burning people out. Although some employees exhibit increased commitment by happily working longer hours, the real payoff comes when employees innovate during the workday. Productivity comes from working smarter, not harder. Creative juices flow when people are excited about their work.

FIGURE 6.13

Sam's Solutions' Increased Productivity and Innovation

Payroll today		$300,000
Increased productivity from less absenteeism		
Assumptions: Percentage of payroll wasted by unplanned absenteeism	2%	
Percent reduction of unplanned absenteeism	20%	$1,200
Increased productivity from telecommuting		
Assumptions: Percentage of additional personnel who telecommute	10%	
Percentage of increased productivity for telecommuters	10%	$3,000
Increased productivity from reduced business travel		
Assumptions: Percentage of additional personnel doing less business travel	5%	
Percentage of increased productivity from less travel	5%	$750
Increased productivity from less unplanned absenteeism, more telecommuting, and less business travel		$4,950
Average percentage gain in productivity of the payroll		1.65%
Increased productivity from green buildings		
Assumptions: Percentage of additional personnel impacted by green buildings	10%	
Percentage of increased productivity from green buildings	10%	
Percent of gain not already counted in other benefits	10%	$300
Increased productivity and innovation from improved collaboration		
Assumptions: Percentage of personnel impacted by better collaboration	10%	
Percentage of increased productivity from collaboration	10%	
Percent of gain not already counted in other benefits	10%	$300
Increased productivity and innovation from higher engagement		
Assumptions: Percentage of personnel more engaged	25%	
Percentage of increased productivity from higher engagement	10%	
Percent of gain not already counted in other benefits	10%	$750
Increased productivity and innovation from green buildings, more collaboration, and higher employee engagement		$1,350
Average percentage gain in productivity of the payroll		0.45%
Increase in overall productivity and innovation in 3 to 5 years		$6,300
Average percentage gain in productivity of the payroll overall		2.10%
Number of full-time equivalent (FTE) employees needed to achieve the same overall gain		0.1

Potential Increased Employee Productivity and Innovation

Figures 6.13 and 6.14 show the six contributors to the productivity and innovation benefit for Sam's Solutions and M&D Corp., respectively. A critical part of these calculations is the base value of the current payroll cost. There are several ways we arrive at this amount.

First, based on US Bureau of Labor Statistics data, total employer compensation costs for private industry workers averaged $28.10 per hour worked in March 2011.[23] About 70% of that compensation cost was for wages and salaries, while 30% was for benefits. The $28.10 an hour is the average of compensation costs in 15 metropolitan areas in the United States, ranging from $41.42 in San Jose–San Francisco–Oakland to $23.29 in Miami–Fort Lauderdale–Pompano Beach. We use an average of $28 per hour in our calculations.

According to OECD statistics, US workers spent an average of 1,768 hours at work in 2009, with a range of 1,801 to 1,796 hours worked per year between 2005 and 2008.[24] If we assume an average of 1,800 hours worked per year at an average compensation cost of $28 per hour, each employee costs a company $50,400 per year. This is close to the $50,787 average annual US wage in OECD data for 2009.[25] We assume $50,000 per year as the average cost per employee in a mid-size company.

According to the World Salaries site, the average income for US manufacturing employees in 2005 was $2,928 per month, or $35,136 per year; office clerks earned $27,768 a year; and retail salespersons earned $27,120.[26] We assume an average salary and wage cost $40,000 per employee in the manufacturing and distribution retail sector, below the $50,000 average.

Calculations based on similar data on the World Salary site indicate that US wages in 2005 for professionals like accountants, chemical engineers, and computer programmers were $97,577, $74,364, and $64,536 respectively. We assume an average cost of $60,000 per employee for the professional services sector for large companies and $50,000 per employee for small services companies, like Sam's Solutions.

We assume that payroll costs are roughly equivalent to 30% of revenue for all companies. Using the above employee pay assumptions, we calculate the number of employees shown for each company in Figures 1.25 and 1.26. We add the modest 2% productivity benefit for Sam's Solutions and M&D Corp. to this base payroll cost, as shown in Figures 6.13 and 6.14.

FIGURE 6.14

M&D Corp.'s Increased Productivity and Innovation

Payroll today		**$150,000,000**
Increased productivity from less absenteeism		
Assumptions: Percentage of payroll wasted by unplanned absenteeism	*2%*	
Percent reduction of unplanned absenteeism	*20%*	$600,000
Increased productivity from telecommuting		
Assumptions: Percentage of additional personnel who telecommute	*10%*	
Percentage of increased productivity for telecommuters	*10%*	$1,500,000
Increased productivity from reduced business travel		
Assumptions: Percentage of additional personnel doing less business travel	*5%*	
Percentage of increased productivity from less travel	*5%*	$375,000
Increased productivity from less unplanned absenteeism, more telecommuting, and less business travel		$2,475,000
Average percentage gain in productivity of the payroll		1.65%
Increased productivity from Green buildings		
Assumptions: Percentage of additional personnel impacted by green buildings	*10%*	
Percentage of increased productivity from green buildings	*10%*	
Percent of gain not already counted in other benefits	*10%*	$150,000
Increased productivity and innovation from improved collaboration		
Assumptions: Percentage of personnel impacted by better collaboration	*10%*	
Percentage of increased productivity from collaboration	*10%*	
Percent of gain not already counted in other benefits	*10%*	$150,000
Increased productivity and innovation from higher engagement		
Assumptions: Percentage of personnel more engaged	*25%*	
Percentage of increased productivity from higher engagement	*10%*	
Percent of gain not already counted in other benefits	*10%*	$375,000
Increased productivity and innovation from green buildings, more collaboration, and higher employee engagement		$675,000
Average percentage gain in productivity of the payroll		0.45%
Increase in overall productivity and innovation in 3 to 5 years		$3,150,000
Average percentage gain in productivity of the payroll overall		2.10%
Number of full-time equivalent (FTE) employees needed to achieve the same overall gain		78.8

BENEFIT 6

Reduced Hiring and Attrition Expenses

*Employees are the key to growth in good times and survival in bad.
If they're on board, they can keep a company afloat and help it prepare
for a stronger future. In these times of low morale, and perhaps because of
the stress of harder economic conditions, many people want more meaning
at work. A green focus will help engage and inspire your people to keep them
going in tough times ... By getting lean on stuff, not on people, you earn
incredible loyalty. Generating excitement around new, green ways of
doing business, finding ways to use less energy and materials, and creating
products and services that help customers reduce their environmental
impacts will keep your people going in hard times and drive profitability.*

— Andrew Winston, *Green Recovery*

The War for Talent Still Rages

If only accountants agree with this CEO maxim: People are our most important asset. Employees are too often pigeonholed as an expense in income statements, rather than as assets on the balance sheet. Nevertheless, employees are vital human capital supporting company success, and companies compete fiercely to attract and retain the best and brightest talent.

In 1997, McKinsey, a management consulting firm, did a landmark study of 77 companies and almost 6,000 managers and executives to assess the importance of this issue. They found that the most important corporate resource over the next 20 years would be talent: smart, sophisticated business people who are technologically literate, globally astute, and operationally innovative. In 2001, McKinsey updated the study and found that, despite the economic slowdown, the war for talent was intensifying dramatically. Their update showed that 89% of those surveyed thought it was more difficult to attract talented people than it had been three years earlier, and 90% thought it was more difficult to retain them. McKinsey concluded that attracting and retaining talent was not just a valid desire — it was a business imperative.

In 2008, a third McKinsey report confirmed that the war for talent still rages.[1] The report summarized findings from two studies. The first, in 2006, indicated that executives regarded finding talented people as the single most important managerial preoccupation for the decade. The second study, conducted in November 2007, revealed that nearly half of the respondents expect intensifying competition for talent — and the increasingly global nature of that competition — to have a major effect on their companies over the next five years. No other global trend was considered nearly as significant. Executives need to create strategies that nurture talent at all levels.

Those value propositions should reflect what prospective employees seek. Figure 7.1 shows that some potential recruits see the organization's values and reputation as differentiators, and Figure 7.2 summarizes indications that a company's sustainability reputation makes a difference. Research published in the *Harvard Business Review* indicates that 75% of US workforce entrants see social responsibility and environmental commitment as important criteria in selecting employers.[2] A poll on MonsterTRAK.com found that 80% of young professionals are interested in securing a job that has a positive impact on the environment, and 92% would be more inclined to work for a company that is environmentally friendly.[3] A good CSR reputation matters to potential recruits.

FIGURE 7.1

Why Employees Join Organizations

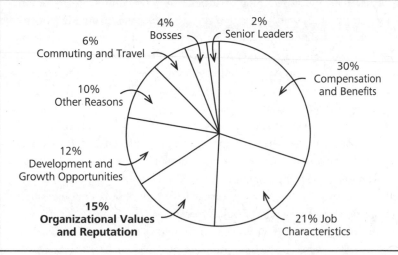

- 2% Senior Leaders
- 4% Bosses
- 6% Commuting and Travel
- 10% Other Reasons
- 12% Development and Growth Opportunities
- **15% Organizational Values and Reputation**
- 21% Job Characteristics
- 30% Compensation and Benefits

Source: Adapted from a slide used by Jay Dorio at a UN Environment Programme: Finance Initiative meeting, March 2011, based on Kenexa's WorkTrends 2010 survey of 10,000 US employees.

FIGURE 7.2

CSR Reputation Attracts Top Talent

40% of MBA grads rate **CSR** as an "extremely" or "very" important company reputation measure when job hunting.
92% of students and entry-level hires seek an environmentally friendly company.

Source: "Facts and Figures about Sustainability" [accessed July 30, 2011], John Molson School of Business, 2011, johnmolson.concordia.ca.

75% of entrants into today's workforce evaluate firms' environmental and social responsibility records prior to choosing an employer of preference.

Source: Jeffrey Hollender, Ashley Orgain, and Ted Nunez, "The Business Case for Sustainability" [accessed July 30, 2011], Kaplan Eduneering/Seventh Generation Sustainability Institute, February 2010, www.institutesustainability.com.

A Sustainable Enterprise Is a Talent Magnet

Hiring top talent is one challenge; keeping it is another. As shown in Figure 7.3, many employees have their periscopes raised to keep an eye out for more attractive corporate shores. However, employees who are highly committed to an organization work hard, are absent less often, and are less likely to leave for a new job. A UK survey found that nearly half that country's workers were more likely to stay with an employer that allowed its workforce to "donate time or raise money for charities during working hours."[4]

Survey after survey shows that the best people stay when they feel like valued contributors to company success, when their innovative ideas are solicited, when a profit-sharing scheme helps them reap personal benefits from their efforts to help the company do well, and when they are empowered, have career opportunities, and feel the company respects work–life balance issues. This is about the G in ESG. Exemplary governance includes human resources policies and practices that bring out the best in people.

For example, LoyaltyOne, the company that operates the Air Miles reward program, was selected as the Best Employer in Canada in 2011 by the *Globe and Mail* "Report on Business" because

- its rate of staff turnover had dropped from 23% in 2008 to 11% in 2009
- the company's "associate engagement score," which measures "the extent to which [employees] are committed, motivated and actively involved in helping the company be successful," had improved from 79% to 85%
- 85% of employees had said they would recommend their employer "as one of the best places to work," up 6% from 2008.[5]

LoyaltyOne attributes its culture of engagement to visible senior-leadership support for its sustainability initiatives; regular broadcasting of sustainability news using internal communication channels; contests with environmentally friendly products as prizes; education to help employees live greener at home; an annual environmental fair where external vendors bring in their catalogues and showcase their green products to staff; management support for grassroots green ideas; and a regular survey on employee engagement to ensure feedback opportunities. Publicity about these efforts helps attract top talent to the company.[6]

Figure 7.4 illustrates how some people are retained by the sustainability dimensions of their companies. Others simply want to stay with a company that cares about its employees and respects them as people. Companies with exemplary sustainability practices are strong magnets for good people.

FIGURE 7.3

One Foot Out the Door

"As many as **two-thirds** of today's workers are either **actively looking for new jobs or merely going through the motions** at their current jobs. While they still show up for work each day, in the ways that count, many have quit."

Employee Priorities

- Keep learning
- Achieve reasonable security
- Be successful
- Ensure work and family flourish
- **Make sure work, as well a life, has meaning**

Source: "Nearly Two-Thirds of US Workers Don't Care about Their Work" [accessed July 30, 2011], press release for Judith Bardwick's *One Foot Out the Door* (AMACOM, 2008), CSRwire.com, November 6, 2007.

FIGURE 7.4

CSR Reputation Retains Top Talent

83% of employees in G7 countries say their company's positive **CSR reputation** increases their **loyalty**
(GlobeScan 2006)

76% of employees are looking for a job at some level, ranging from casually surfing the Internet to actively interviewing.
(The Vargas Group, 2007)

Only **24%** of employees report they feel "truly loyal" to their employers and plan to stay at least two years.
(The Vargas Group, 2007)

57% of employees say their company's CSR reputation is a factor in retaining them.
(Towers Perrin-ISR global survey, 2007)

Paying the Price for Voluntary Turnover

Involuntary turnover happens when companies downsize or encourage employees to find a better fit for their skills somewhere else. Voluntary turnover occurs when good people decide to leave, sometimes moving to competitors who lure them away. Voluntary turnover costs a company dearly. To calculate the cost, we multiply the number of employees who leave voluntarily each year by the costs associated with their leaving and replacement.

According to Compdata surveys of 5,300 participating HR departments, the average turnover rate in 2008 in the United States was 16.5% for the manufacturing sector, 24.4% for the distribution and warehousing sector, and 19.8% for the services sector, with an average of 18.7% for all sectors. More importantly for this discussion, the voluntary turnover rates were 10.4% for the manufacturing sector, 14.9% for the distribution and warehousing sector, and 14% for the services sector, with an average of 12.5% for all sectors.[7] We conservatively assume a 12% voluntary turnover rate for both M&D Corp. and Sam's Solutions.

Estimates of the total cost of turnover range from 30% of the yearly salary of the vacated position for hourly employees to as much as 150%.[8] Some HR professionals estimate this turnover cost between 50% and 125% of an employee's salary.[9] These estimates account for direct and indirect costs incurred before the employee leaves, while the job is vacant, during the hiring and on-boarding process, and during the formal and informal training periods. They include productivity hits to the leaving employee, co-workers, and management before the departure; lost productivity while the job is vacant and being covered off by colleagues or managers; and further productivity losses by these people as the new person is trained and gets up to speed. Other costs are personnel processing costs, advertising expenses, replacement agency costs, and the difficult-to-estimate longer-term cost of lost experience and lost relationships with important contacts. We conservatively estimate that the cost to replace an employee who leaves voluntarily is 40% of the salary of the departing employees.

Figures 7.5 and 7.6 show the calculations for the cost of voluntary turnover at Sam's Solutions and M&D Corp. All assumptions are conservative, including the anticipation that the company's commitment to sustainability would retain 25% of those who might otherwise consider leaving the company. A company's sustainability strategies, behaviors, and reputation can save it considerable involuntary turnover expense.

FIGURE 7.5

Sam's Solutions' Savings on Voluntary Turnover

Number of personnel	6
Assumption: Percentage of employees who voluntarily leave each year	*12%*
Number of personnel who voluntarily leave each year	0.7
Average employee salary	$50,000
Assumption: Equivalent percentage of an average salary needed to cover direct and indirect costs incurred before the employee leaves, while the job is vacant, during the hiring and on-boarding process, and during the formal and informal training period	*40%*
Cost of losing and replacing one employee who leaves voluntarily	$20,000
Cost of losing and replacing all employees who leave voluntarily	$14,400
Assumption: Percentage of departing personnel who would not leave because they are attracted to the company's sustainability reputation	*25%*
Savings from lower voluntary turnover rate because of sustainability reputation	$3,600

FIGURE 7.6

M&D Corp.'s Savings on Voluntary Turnover

Number of personnel	3,750
Assumption: Percentage of employees who voluntarily leave each year	*12%*
Number of personnel who voluntarily leave each year	450
Average employee salary	$40,000
Assumption: Equivalent percentage of an average salary needed to cover direct and indirect costs incurred before the employee leaves, while the job is vacant, during the hiring and on-boarding process, and during the formal and informal training period	*40%*
Cost of losing and replacing one employee who leaves voluntarily	$16,000
Cost of losing and replacing all employees who leave voluntarily	$7,200,000
Assumption: Percentage of departing personnel who would not leave because they are attracted to the company's sustainability reputation	*25%*
Savings from lower voluntary turnover rate because of sustainability reputation	$1,800,000

Reduced Risks

*Looking for environmental risks requires going far beyond the traditional
company boundaries. Risks may arise from upstream (with suppliers)
or downstream (with customers) ... At the nuts-and-bolts level, identifying
enterprise risk means understanding exactly how a company affects the
environment and how the constraints of nature affect the company.*

— Daniel C. Esty and Andrew S. Winston, *Green to Gold*

Standard Two-Part Business Case

There are only two reasons a company changes: it wants to capture opportunities and/or it wants to mitigate risks. That is, it is attracted to the carrot and/or it wants to avoid the stick. Convincing a company to fully embed sustainability into its strategies and operations therefore requires a compelling two-part business case. This case must include the risks of what might happen if the company does not take action, as well as the benefits it can reap if it does.

A successful company's carefully crafted strategies, operational processes, and product lines have served it well. There have to be very good reasons to mess with success. Sustainability champions need to show what the company will gain if it embraces sustainability-related strategies — which is what we have done with the first six benefits — *and* they need to articulate the threats to the company if it does not.

Later, when senior leaders explain why they did the right things and are reaping the benefits, they may deconstruct the original drivers and emphasize the opportunities that they wanted to capture by instituting new environmental, social, and governance strategies and procedures. They often downplay the risks they wanted to avoid, but these risks were usually critical motivators.

Figure 8.1 shows the benefits reaped from smart sustainability strategies aligned with the "Capture Opportunities" part of the business case. The benefit of avoiding the risk of not being proactive on sustainability issues is aligned with the "Avoid Risks" component. Do not be deceived by the 6:1 ratio of upsides to downside. In the decision-making process, this weighting ratio may be reversed.

In financial reports, the income statement and balance sheet provide a rearview mirror snapshot of past performance. Management's discussion and analysis (MD&A) in the annual report is where management looks at future prospects. The risk section of the MD&A explains how various uncertain non-financial factors could significantly impact future success. This chapter fills that role in this book. We identify salient risks for companies that do not seize the sustainability imperative, assign probabilities of the risks happening in the next three to five years, and extrapolate the potential impacts on the profit-and-loss / income statement, as shown in Figure 8.2.

In a sales situation, we sometimes use the FUD factor — planting seeds of fear, uncertainty, and doubt about what could happen if the proposed solution is not adopted. The risks help show that the status quo is not a viable option. This chapter provides the FUD factor for the sustainability business case.

FIGURE 8.1

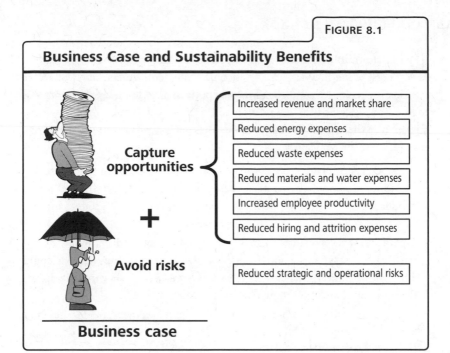

Business Case and Sustainability Benefits

Capture
opportunities

| Increased revenue and market share |
| Reduced energy expenses |
| Reduced waste expenses |
| Reduced materials and water expenses |
| Increased employee productivity |
| Reduced hiring and attrition expenses |

+

Avoid risks

| Reduced strategic and operational risks |

Business case

FIGURE 8.2

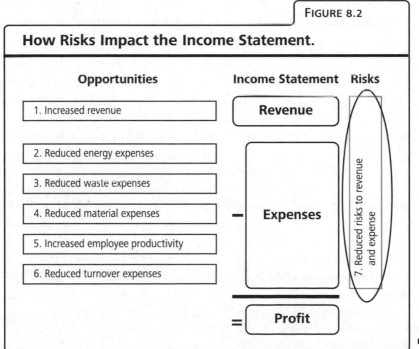

How Risks Impact the Income Statement.

| Opportunities | Income Statement | Risks |

1. Increased revenue — **Revenue**

2. Reduced energy expenses

3. Reduced waste expenses

4. Reduced material expenses — **Expenses**

5. Increased employee productivity

6. Reduced turnover expenses

7. Reduced risks to revenue and expense

= **Profit**

Four Categories of Risk

R isks slip into the board room in several costumes. Some are scarier than others. Some may impact the income statement; others may jeopardize multiple aspects of the company's financial performance. Some are more material than others. When performing sustainability risk management (SRM), we pay attention to the same four categories of risks that are assessed in enterprise risk management (ERM) scenarios:

- **Strategic risks** relate to the company's future business plans and strategies, including reputational risks associated with its markets and demand for its products and services, competitive threats, technology and product innovation risks, and risks arising from public policy.
- **Operational risks** relate to factors that threaten the effectiveness of the company's people, systems, and processes, as well as external events that could affect the operation of its businesses and its bottom line. They include threats from supply chain and product life-cycle impacts.
- **Compliance risks** relate to the possibility that government regulatory actions will impose additional costs on the company or force it to change its business models or practices in order to be compliant.
- **Financial risk** relates to the company's ability to meet financial obligations and mitigate credit risk, liquidity risk, and exposure to financial market risks.

Ernst and Young's 2010 Business Risk Report summarized business risks identified by a panel of 70 executives representing 14 industry sectors. Figure 8.3 arrays the report's top 10 risks into the risk quadrants listed above. For the first time in E&Y's annual survey, "social acceptance risk and corporate social responsibility" was a top 10 business risk. "Radical greening" also made the list, suggesting stakeholder demands for more proactive measures to reduce environmental impacts. The report also found that companies are threatened by changes in regulations and carbon trading schemes.

Interestingly, the executives identified 15 "below the radar" risks, in this priority sequence: inability to innovate, emerging technologies, taxation risk, pricing pressures, resource scarcity, shifts in consumer demands, global realignment, reputation risks, energy shocks, supply chain and "extraprise" risks, new business models, capital allocation changes, intermediary power shifts, and shifting demographics. That is quite an exhaustive/exhausting list of executive sleep-disrupters.

Our premise is that sustainability strategies help mitigate risks from all of the above 25 risks, avoiding threats to revenue and increases to expenses.

FIGURE 8.3

Top 10 Business Risks of 2010

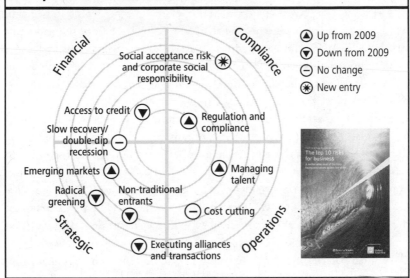

- ▲ Up from 2009
- ▼ Down from 2009
- ⊖ No change
- ✳ New entry

Financial

Compliance

Social acceptance risk and corporate social responsibility ✳

Access to credit ▼

Regulation and compliance ▲

Slow recovery/ double-dip ⊖ recession

Emerging markets ▲

Managing talent ▲

Radical greening ▼

Non-traditional entrants ▼

Cost cutting ⊖

Strategic

Executing alliances and transactions ▼

Operations

Source: Adpated from "The Top 10 Risks for Global Business," Ernst & Young Business Risk Report 2010, July 2010, p. 3. Based on interviews with 70 industry executives and analysts in14 industry sectors.

Mitigating Strategic Risks That Could Erode Revenue

A business is perceived as legitimate when its activities align with the goals and values of the society in which it operates. In other words, to be legitimate, a business must earn its social license to operate from its important stakeholders. To this end, a company tries to create and maintain its image as a good corporate citizen, or at least a better one than its competitors. Companies may justify their sustainability initiatives as a means of boosting their legitimacy, brand image, and reputation. Strategic risks threaten the company's reputation, which could impact its future revenue and, in turn, its long-term profitability.

Regulatory and litigation risks are usually top of mind when companies think of sustainability-related risks, and most companies have learned how to avoid or manage them. The new kid on the block — reputation risk — may grow to be the most important for many businesses. Why? The big guys are becoming more aggressive with their suppliers and demanding transparency on the energy, carbon, water, material, and social footprints of not only purchased products but also the supplier's whole company.

Walmart led this trend in 2010 with a 15 question survey of its 100,000 suppliers (see Figure 2.2), and now companies like Procter & Gamble are following suit with their supply chains. Other retailers like Safeway and Best Buy are showing interest in adopting similar supplier-rating schemes. A firm's ability to satisfy the sustainability criteria of these big corporations could be a gating factor for its continued income from these business-to-business (B2B) customers. Companies that do not improve their track record and associated reputations could be jeopardizing revenue streams. The bar is being raised. Although it may be shiny today, the corporate image may tarnish from lack of polishing.

Figures 8.4 and 8.5 summarize the potential hits to revenue from seven threats. Five of them arise from potential brand erosion on environmental footprint issues; one is based on lack of action to mitigate escalating energy, water, and material expenses; and the last is the threat of sudden disruption of the company's supply chain or access to customers. There are other potential threats, but this is a reasonable cross-sector starter set. In each case, the risk is calculated by monetizing its potential impact and factoring that amount by the likelihood it will occur within our three- to five-year horizon. In the next few pages we elaborate on these threats to sustainability laggards' revenue.

FIGURE 8.4

Sam's Solutions' Potential Revenue Loss from Strategic Risks (Base revenue $1,000,000)

	Percent of Revenue at Risk	Percent Probability of Occurring Within 3 to 5 Years	Potential Lost Revenue
Risk to revenue from poor reputation on energy and carbon management	5%	25%	$12,500
Risk to revenue from poor reputation on water management	5%	25%	$12,500
Risk to revenue from poor reputation on materials and waste management	5%	20%	$10,000
Risk to revenue from poor supplier reputation and behaviors	5%	10%	$5,000
Risk to revenue from poor reputation on ecosystem damages	5%	1%	$500
Risk to revenue from less competitive prices	10%	10%	$10,000
Risk to revenue from sudden disruptions in the value chain	2%	5%	$1,000
Potential decreased revenue without sustainability initiatives			**$51,500**

FIGURE 8.5

M&D Corp.'s Potential Revenue Loss from Strategic Risks (Base revenue $500,000,000)

	Percent of Revenue at Risk	Percent Probability of Occurring Within 3 to 5 Years	Potential Lost Revenue
Risk to revenue from poor reputation on energy and carbon management	5%	25%	$6,250,000
Risk to revenue from poor reputation on water management	5%	25%	$6,250,000
Risk to revenue from poor reputation on materials and waste management	5%	20%	$5,000,000
Risk to revenue from poor supplier reputation and behaviors	5%	10%	$2,500,000
Risk to revenue from poor reputation on ecosystem damages	5%	1%	$250,000
Risk to revenue from less competitive prices	10%	10%	$5,000,000
Risk to revenue from sudden disruptions in the value chain	2%	5%	$500,000
Potential decreased revenue without sustainability initiatives			**$25,750,000**

Risk to Revenue from Poor Reputation on Energy and Carbon Management

Companies share stakeholder concerns about the multiple repercussions of climate change, shown in Figure 8.12. The cumulative impact of employee expectations, investor requests, and customer expectations makes carbon a strategic issue for companies today. As can be seen in Figure 8.6, "brand improvement," "product differentiation," and "risk management" are strong reasons for corporate action on climate change. Not only does a company want to grow its revenue using the sustainability strategies described in the chapter on Benefit 1, but it also needs to protect the top-line growth from climate-related reputational threats.

Corporate press releases almost always accompany announcements of reduced energy use with information about associated carbon footprint reductions, since fossil fuels power a substantial proportion of the electricity grid. In most jurisdictions, carbon reductions do not save the company money ... yet. When a price is put on carbon through a carbon tax or a cap-and-trade mechanism, companies will reap financial benefit from their carbon reductions. In the meantime, carbon reductions are a proxy for the company's smart governance — it anticipates a price on carbon and is positioning itself strategically to benefit from it rather than being blindsided by it. Energy conservation saves expenses; carbon management builds reputation.

How many business-to-consumer (B2C) and/or B2B customers care enough about climate change and carbon footprints to use them as supplier criteria? Increasingly, procurement criteria include a significant weighting for carbon management in B2B transactions. Firms supplying public sector organizations, like the US government's General Services Administration procurement arm, or large retail firms like Walmart, feel increasing pressure from carbon-linked or sustainability procurement criteria, which account for as much as 15% of the proposal evaluation weighting, up from 5% a few years ago.[1]

We conservatively assume a company could lose 5% of its revenue if B2C and B2B customers are not happy with its action to reduce its carbon contribution to the climate change threat. Further, we conservatively assume there is a 25% chance that customers will vote with their wallets on companies and products that they perceive to be harming the health of the planet. The resulting risk to revenue for our two sample companies is shown in Figures 8.4 and 8.5.

FIGURE 8.6

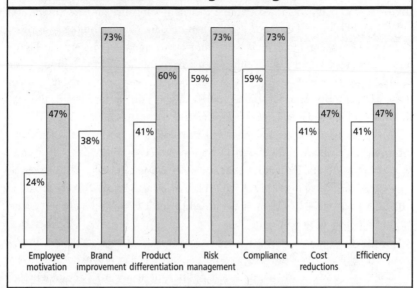

Reasons for Climate Change Strategies

Source: Adapted from Environmental Leader, "Reason for Corporate Climate Change Strategy (% of respondents)" in *Environmental and Energy Data Book Q2 2011,* July 2011, p. 24. Based on Carbon Disclosure Project data, 2011.

Risk to Revenue from Poor Reputation on Water Management

Industries are being held accountable for their water use and treatment, not only by regulatory agencies, but also by shareholders, NGOs, and the communities in which they operate. As the first four environmental concerns in Figure 8.7 confirm, water is now the dominant environmental issue in the minds of the public. It is increasingly called "the next carbon," but — unlike carbon — water is the world's most critical resource, more vital than oil. Water sustains life and, thus, the global food chain. Water issues become real personal, real fast.

All industries need to understand critical issues such as peak water, water footprinting, and embedded water in both products and services.[2] How companies address, or fail to address, these concerns may increasingly be seen as a matter of fiduciary duty. Yet in its 2011 analysis of Global 2000 companies, EIRIS found that 54% of them are exposed to water risks, but only 9.7% have set water quality targets.[3]

There are two ways that water issues can jeopardize revenue. First, how a company manages its water usage affects its image as a good corporate citizen. A company's brand is damaged when public questions arise about whether the company properly addresses issues of sustainable and equitable water use. Reducing a firm's water footprint is a way to mitigate reputational risk and protect the inclination of customers to continue to do business with a water-responsible company.

Secondly, water shortages may affect a company's ability to make its products. If it cannot produce its goods, it cannot sell them. Companies in every sector may increasingly face freshwater shortages in their supply chain or their own operations. Water shortages pose higher risks to heavy water users in the food and beverage, semiconductor manufacturing, power generation, manufacturing, and extractive industry sectors. In 2009, Nestlé Waters abandoned a plan to build the United States' largest bottling plant in California, and Coca-Cola lost its license to operate in India for three years in the wake of droughts.[4] PepsiCo hopes to achieve a long-term goal of zero water intake at its largest facilities by developing a technology that removes the water from potatoes so it can be used in the company's factories.[5]

We conservatively assume that poor reputation on water management, and water dependence, could threaten 5% of the revenue in laggard companies that are not on track to being water neutral. There is a 25% chance this will happen. The resulting risk of revenue erosion is quantified in Figures 8.4 and 8.5.

FIGURE 8.7

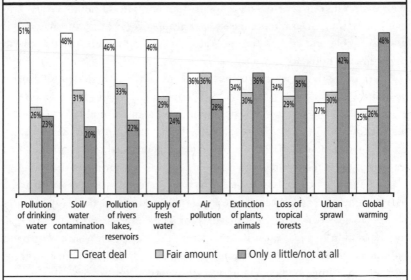

Public Concern about Environmental Issues

□ Great deal   ▦ Fair amount   ▥ Only a little/not at all

Source: Adapted from "Public Perceptions of Environmental Issues, March 2011 (% of US Adults)" [accessed July 30, 2011], EnvironmentalLeader.com/charts. Based on Gallup survey, March 2011.

Risk to Revenue from Poor Reputation on Materials and Waste Management

We are running out of resources as we eat into our natural capital rather than living off its interest. Our rapacious industrial appetite for finite raw materials is not sustainable, and as they become scarcer, increasingly aggressive tactics will be required to find and extract them.

One of the ways in which a company's reputation can be sullied is by direct or indirect involvement in the abuse of people, especially indigenous people, who get in the way of resource extraction. As well, environmental pollution is often a companion of desperate efforts to find, mine, and refine vital materials. Reputation-destroying news stories about these social and environmental impacts can lead to customers going elsewhere for their products and services.

These are the material- and waste-related reputational threats that start at the source of the materials. As shown in Figure 1.10, our take-make-waste business model provides two more opportunities for waste issues to damage a company's reputation in the eyes of its customers. It can cause air, water, or ground pollution around its refining, manufacturing, or commercial building site — overflowing tailing ponds are in this waste category. A company can also be held accountable for the responsible disposal of the product after the user is finished with it. Images of full-up landfill sites and of Asian children picking through mountains of e-waste have sensitized customers to these waste issues. As can be seen by the bars in Figure 8.8, hazardous waste is such a concern for companies that they are often quiet about their goals to reduce it, as reduction goals imply that they have hazardous waste in the first place. Sustainability strategies promote responsible material and waste management, closed-loop systems, and product take-back by producers. These material-neutral approaches reduce the need to extract new natural resources and, therefore, reduce the associated waste from exploration, mining and drilling, refining, and processing steps before the raw materials arrive at the company's receiving dock.

Laggard companies are more exposed to hits to their reputation from materials and waste issues. Conservatively, we assume that 5% of the company's annual revenue is at risk if it has a poor reputation on material and waste management, and there is a 20% chance that revenue could be lost in the next three to five years because customers go elsewhere. The resulting negative impact on revenue is calculated for Sam's Solutions and M&D Corp. in Figures 8.4 and 8.5.

FIGURE 8.8

Most Popular Sustainability Goals

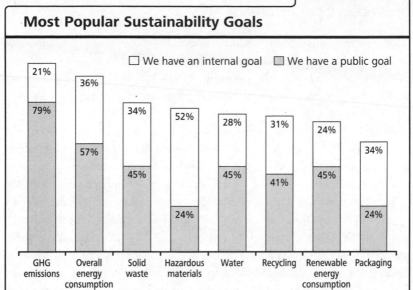

☐ We have an internal goal ☐ We have a public goal

GHG emissions	21% / 79%	
Overall energy consumption	36% / 57%	
Solid waste	34% / 45%	
Hazardous materials	52% / 24%	
Water	28% / 45%	
Recycling	31% / 41%	
Renewable energy consumption	24% / 45%	
Packaging	34% / 24%	

Source: Adapted from Environmental Leader, "Most Popular Sustainability Goals (% of companies)" in *Environmental and Energy Data Book Q2 2011*, July 2011, p. 28. Based on Green Research's Sustainability Executive Survey data, June 2011.

Risk to Revenue from Poor Reputations of Suppliers or Customers

No longer are companies expected to report only on their own operations; now they are also held accountable for the operations of their suppliers. When a company's reputation is only as good as the reputation of the worst-behaving supplier in its supply chain, its executives become very focused on avoiding any guilt by association.

Nike and Gap were the early sacrificial lambs on the altar of corporate accountability when conditions in offshore sweatshops producing their goods caused controversy. Recently, Apple was taken to task for conditions in its suppliers' plants in China (see Figure 8.9). In June 2011, Greenpeace accused toy manufacturers such as Mattel and Walt Disney of packaging their Barbie dolls in material from Indonesian rainforests, thereby contributing to the country's rapid deforestation and pushing critically endangered wildlife, including tigers, toward extinction.[6] In contrast, in May 2011, SC Johnson added its name to the growing list of companies pledging to source sustainable palm oil. Like Walmart, General Mills, and McDonald's, SC Johnson set a goal of using palm oil only from certified sustainable sources by 2015.[7] These companies knew their corporate images would be at risk if Malaysian farmers seeking more land for palm trees destroyed ecosystems and animal habitats.

As Arthur Andersen learned the hard way, the reputation of a significant customer can deal a fatal blow to your revenue stream. When other customers learned about the accounting firm's involvement in the Enron fiasco, its income dried up and it dropped off the corporate landscape.

In many ways, the Internet is responsible for the increased importance of corporate reputation. The Internet makes it easy to communicate internationally and to instantly organize individuals into large and significant global groups. This has dramatically changed the power dynamic between corporations and citizens. Risks related to sustainability are potential flash points, as consumers test their new-found ability to rally support for activist causes. A company can lose its reputation overnight as a result of poor reputation management, especially in its supply chain.

We estimate that 5% of a company's annual revenue could be jeopardized by its suppliers' or customers' socially and/or environmentally irresponsible behaviors. Conservatively assuming a 10% probability of being shunned for this reason, revenue at risk for our two hypothetical companies is calculated in Figures 8.4 and 8.5.

FIGURE 8.9

Apple in China

In 2011, the Beijing-based non-profit Institute of Public and Environmental Affairs (IPE) accused Apple of ignoring health and environmental concerns at the Chinese factories of its suppliers. In its ranking of 29 tech companies, IPE placed Apple last.

"[Apple] only care about the price and quality [of their products] and not the environmental and social responsibility issues. In some ways they drive the suppliers to cut corners to win their contracts," IPE director Ma Jun told Reuters.

According to IPE, workers at the Wintek plant, where touch-screens for Apple products are produced, became ill from n-hexane exposure. Wintek eventually removed the substance after being sued by workers. IPE said Apple ignored workers' concerns, but the company also did not acknowledge that Wintek was a supplier. By refusing to confirm who its suppliers were, Apple "avoided responsibility for environmental problems in its supply chain."

IPE was also critical of Apple's lack of response to worker suicides at the Foxconn plant. The same month the report was released, a 25-year-old Foxconn employee died, becoming at least the 14th suicide victim at the plant in a 12-month period.

Source: "Apple Ranks Last for Environmental Response" [accessed July 30, 2011], Environmentalleader.com, January 24, 2011.

Risk to Revenue from Poor Reputation on Ecosystem Damages

Ecosystem services are the benefits people gain from nature and biodiversity. These include water, crops, timber, flood protection, waste assimilation, carbon sequestration, recreation, and spiritual benefits. What are nature's life-support services worth? In one sense, they are priceless. The Earth's economies would soon collapse without fertile soil, fresh water, breathable air, and an amenable climate. But "priceless" too often translates to "zero" in the equations that guide land use and policy decisions. Ecological economists believe more concrete numbers are required. In one of the first efforts to calculate a global number, a team of researchers from the United States, Argentina, and the Netherlands put an average price tag of $33 trillion a year on these fundamental ecosystem services. As shown in Figure 8.10, that is nearly twice the value of the global gross national product (GNP) of US$18 trillion.

In a groundbreaking corporate *environmental* profit-and-loss statement in 2011, the shoe and sportswear company Puma estimated it would have to pay $133 million a year to cover its impacts on water and climate, the two largest sources of global environmental costs (as shown in Figure 8.11). Puma's direct operations were responsible for about $10 million; its supply chain was responsible for $123 million. Puma's P&L statement will eventually include other environmental impacts, such as the cost of waste and land use, as well as its social and economic impact in such areas as job creation, taxes, and philanthropy.[8] Reporting trends foreshadow regulations. Puma prepared its statement in case such disclosure becomes a requirement.

Accounting standards organizations are discussing new rules that could require businesses to publish information on their environmental and social impacts along with their financial statements. In 2011, the World Business Council for Sustainable Development published a *Guide to Corporate Ecosystem Valuation*, which would help companies begin to assess the cost of their damage to ecosystems. The World Resources Institute published the "Corporate Ecosystem Services Review" as a companion document.

A study from environmental research group Trucost estimated the cost of environmental damage by the 3,000 biggest companies in the world as about $2.2 trillion in 2008.[9] That figure equals 6% to 7% of the companies' average revenue. We assume 5% of a company's revenue could be at risk when the public learns of its externalized cost of damages to vital ecosystems. Assuming an ultra-conservative 1% possibility of this nascent impact being internalized in the next three to five years, Figures 8.4 and 8.5 show the potential cost of ecosystem damage to Sam's Solutions and M&D Corp.

FIGURE 8.10

Value of Ecosystem Services

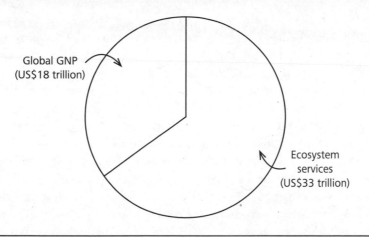

Global GNP
(US$18 trillion)

Ecosystem
services
(US$33 trillion)

Source: Adapted from R. Costanza et al., "The Value of the World's Ecosystem Services and Natural Capital," *Nature,* 387, 1997, p. 256, Table 2.

FIGURE 8.11

Cost of External Ecosystem Damage

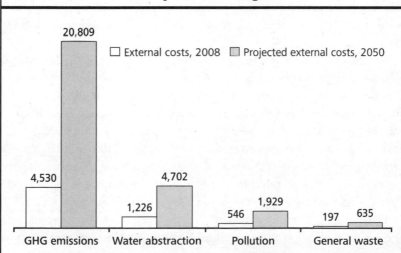

20,809

☐ External costs, 2008   ▨ Projected external costs, 2050

4,530

4,702

1,226

1,929

546

197   635

GHG emissions   Water abstraction   Pollution   General waste

Source: Adapted from Environmental Leader, "Environmental Costs for Global Corporate Economy, 2008 and Projections for 2050 (US$ billions)" in *Environmental and Energy Data Book Q2 2011,* July 2011, p.37. Based UN Environmental Programme data.

Risk to Revenue from Less Competitive Prices

No margin, no mission. Social responsibility and sustainability include growing sufficient revenue and profitability to sustain the organization's mission. There is nothing wrong with building enough margin into the prices of products to generate healthy profits. However, there are two ways a company could jeopardize its margin.

First, it is one thing to be expensive; it is another to be more expensive than competitors. Figure 8.12 shows the concerns that drive companies' climate change strategies. Pricing worries are behind the top three. If competitors are quicker to harvest the benefits of materials, energy, and water efficiencies, they could gain a price advantage and attract customers away.

Second, there is also evidence in the consumer goods retail sector that a business could be leaving margin on the table, or on its competitor's table, if it does not invest in a good CSR reputation. A 2010 study of 3,000 grocery shoppers showed that four dimensions of CSR performance positively influenced consumers' attitudes toward a retailer: environmental friendliness, treating employees fairly, community support, and sourcing from local growers and suppliers. Grocers who offered locally sourced products and who were known to pay their employees fairly earned their customers' goodwill and loyalty. If a retailer was able to improve consumers' perception of its fair treatment of employees and its local sourcing by 20%, the amount of business from those customers increased by 1.7% and 2% respectively. These numbers appear small, but they represent a sales increase of 10% to 15% for the average retailer in the study.[10]

The big surprise in the study was that if a retailer chose to leverage its improved CSR perception into higher prices rather than more sales, a 20% increase in customers' perception of employee fairness "translated to a price premium of about 12%, and a similar increase in local product sourcing translated to a price premium of about 16%. Consumers do not just respond to the price charged; they also respond to how *fair* they think the price is. High prices are considered fairer if they can be attributed to 'good' motives like covering the cost of CSR efforts rather than to 'bad' motives like pure profit-taking."[11]

We conservatively assume that companies not practicing good CSR could find themselves with a price disadvantage that jeopardizes 10% of their revenue. There is a 10% chance of this occurring. Figures 8.4 and 8.5 show the impact on Sam's Solutions and M&D Corp. revenues from this scenario.

FIGURE 8.12

Climate Change-Related Risks

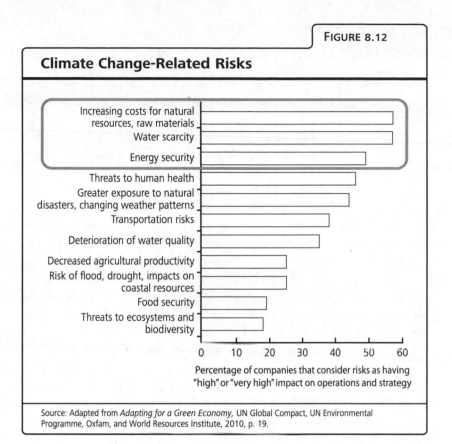

Percentage of companies that consider risks as having
"high" or "very high" impact on operations and strategy

Source: Adapted from *Adapting for a Green Economy,* UN Global Compact, UN Environmental
Programme, Oxfam, and World Resources Institute, 2010, p. 19.

Risk to Revenue from
Sudden Disruptions in the Value Chain

Every company faces a particular set of physical and operational risks from severe weather, political uprisings, protracted permit delays, or other snags in its value chain.

Extreme weather events are happening more frequently, can damage the company's facilities, and may require extensive time and money to rectify. The homes of employees may be severely damaged, or infrastructure providing access to the company site may be destroyed. Supply chain resilience after severe weather events is a growing issue for companies with far-flung global operations and suppliers. Storms at supplier locations or en route can jeopardize supply and force the company to use more expensive alternative sources. The excerpt in Figure 8.13 from Chiquita's 10-K report provides insights into how adverse weather conditions can severely curtail a food company's supply. Work in process may be destroyed. The supplier's own supply chain may be disrupted. And so on. Weather-related supply chain disruptions cause revenue flow disruptions.

At the other end of the value chain, customers who are affected by weather may be in no position to require further products. They may be just trying to survive and rebuild. If the company has not diversified its revenue streams, prompted by sustainability product and service opportunities, the resulting loss of revenue could be financially catastrophic, even though the company's own facilities are unaffected by severe weather.

Replace "severe weather event" in the preceding paragraphs with "rioting in the streets" and the arguments apply equally well. If a company's suppliers and/ or customers have been disrupted by natural disasters or civil unrest, we assume the top-line loss is 2% of revenue. To be extra conservative, we lump in revenue lost when permit approvals are delayed because of the company's problematic track record on environmental and social responsibility.

What are the odds of these disruptions or delays occurring? Of course, it is difficult to say. The frequency and severity of natural and political disasters seems to be increasing. Permit-granting bodies are more stringent about ensuring the company's social license to operate passes muster. Nevertheless, we conservatively assume that the probability that the revenue stream will be interrupted is only 5%.

The results of these assumptions for Sam's Solutions and M&D Corp. are shown in Figures 8.4 and 8.5.

FIGURE 8.13

Chiquita's Supply Chain Challenges

"Our results of operations have been significantly impacted in the past by a variety of weather-related events. For example, as a result of flooding which affected some of our owned farms in Costa Rica and Panama in December 2008, we incurred approximately $33 million of higher costs, including logistics costs, related to rehabilitating the farms and procuring replacement fruit from other sources.

"Although we maintain insurance to cover certain weather-related losses, insurance does not cover all weather-related events and, even when an event is covered, our retention or deductible may be significant. We attempt to pass on some of the incremental costs to customers through contract price increases or temporary price surcharges, but there can be no assurance regarding the extent to which we may be able to pass on uninsured costs in the future. To the extent that climate changes lead to more frequent or more severe adverse weather conditions or events, this could increase the impact on our operations and those of our competitors as described below.

"Bananas, lettuce and other produce can be affected by drought, temperature extremes, hurricanes, windstorms and floods; floods in particular may affect bananas, which are typically grown in tropical lowland areas ... Unfavorable growing conditions caused by these factors can reduce both crop size and crop quality. In extreme cases, entire harvests may be lost. These factors may result in lower sales volume and, in the case of farms we own or manage, increased costs due to expenditures for additional agricultural techniques or agrichemicals, the repair of infrastructure, and the replanting of damaged or destroyed crops. Incremental costs also may be incurred if we need to find alternate short-term supplies of bananas, lettuce or other produce from other growers.

"From time to time, we have experienced shipping interruptions, port damage and changes in shipping routes as a result of weather-related disruptions. While we believe we are adequately insured and would attempt to transport our products by alternative means if we were to experience an interruption, an extended interruption in our ability to ship and distribute our products could have a material adverse effect on us."

Source: "Chiquita Brands International, Form 10-K," United States Securities and Exchange Commission, February 19, 2010, p. 13.

Mitigating Operational Risks
That Could Increase Expenses

Most companies are already familiar with operational-risk management (ORM) and are taking steps to ensure company-wide operational continuity. ORM is the systematic process of planning for, identifying, analyzing, monitoring, responding to, and mitigating operational risks. It involves processes, tools, and techniques that help maximize the probability and results of positive events and minimize the probability and consequences of adverse events. Risks associated with sustainability aspects of the company's operations are simply a special subset of operational risks.

Integrating sustainability considerations into an operational risk program enhances an organization's ability to be competitive in the marketplace, since it enables management to make strategic business decisions based on a more complete and integrated risk portfolio. In order to maintain a competitive advantage and improve overall performance, organizations seek ways to understand and proactively manage the risks that can impact business expenses. Sometimes a company may decide the cost of taking action to avoid the risk is disproportionate to the benefit it receives. By calculating the size of the hit it is prepared to absorb, the company determines its appetite for operational risk.

Sustainability strategies can mitigate several types of operational risk. We look at seven.

1. Risk of higher cost of energy
2. Risk of a price on carbon
3. Risk of higher cost of waste
4. Risk of higher cost of water and materials
5. Risk of higher cost of capital for long-term debt
6. Risk of higher voluntary turnover of employees
7. Risk of lower employee productivity

These risks are monetized for Sam's Solutions and M&D Corp. in Figures 8.14 and 8.15. As with the strategic risks outlined above, we first quantify the potential impact of each risk on expenses and then factor that amount by the likelihood it will occur within the next three to five years. The thinking behind the calculation is explained in the following subsections. All assumptions are educated guesses, as with any planning exercise. The beauty of the Sustainability Advantage Simulator Worksheets and Dashboard at sustsinabilityadvantage.com is that executive judgment calls on these factors can tailor the operational risk assessment to each company's situation.

FIGURE 8.14

Sam's Solutions' Operational Risk of Escalating Expenses

	Base	Percent Potential Impact	Percent Probability Within 3 to 5 Years	Potential Increased Expenses
Risk of higher cost of energy (Base = Cost today)	$20,000	10%	75%	$1,500
Risk of a price on carbon (Base = $20/T x 300T/$1M revenue today)	$6,000	100%	25%	$1,500
Risk of higher cost of waste (Base = Cost today)	$25,000	5%	75%	$938
Risk of higher cost of water and materials (Base = Cost today)	$50,000	5%	75%	$1,875
Risk of higher cost of capital (Base = Long-term debt today)	$300,000	0.60%	75%	$1,350
Risk of higher employee voluntary turnover (Base = Cost today)	$14,400	5%	25%	$180
Risk of lower employee productivity (Base = Total salaries today)	$300,000	1%	10%	$300
Potential increased expenses without sustainability initiatives				**$7,643**

FIGURE 8.15

M&D Corp.'s Operational Risk of Escalating Expenses

	Base	Percent Potential Impact	Percent Probability Within 3 to 5 Years	Potential Increased Expenses
Risk of higher cost of energy (Base = Cost today)	$10,000,000	10%	75%	$750,000
Risk of a price on carbon (Base = $20/T x 300T/$1M revenue today)	$3,000,000	100%	25%	$750,000
Risk of higher cost of waste (Base = Cost today)	$75,000,000	5%	75%	$2,812,500
Risk of higher cost of water and materials (Base = Cost today)	$150,000,000	5%	75%	$5,625,000
Risk of higher cost of capital (Base = Long-term debt today)	$150,000,000	0.60%	75%	$675,000
Risk of higher employee voluntary turnover (Base = Cost today)	$7,200,000	5%	25%	$90,000
Risk of lower employee productivity) (Base = Total salaries today)	$150,000,000	1%	10%	$150,000
Potential increased expenses without sustainability initiatives				**$10,852,500**

Risk of Higher Cost of Energy

When Deloitte polled 400 business decision-makers responsible for their company's energy decisions or energy policy for its *reSources 2011* survey, 60% thought electricity prices would rise by at least 6% in the next one to two years.[12] In 2011, the Institute for Building Efficiency surveyed 4,000 owners and property managers of commercial buildings on six continents. A full 80% of respondents expected energy prices to rise 11% in the coming year.[13] Energy prices are going up. The only questions are "How much?" and "How soon?"

As shown in Figures 8.16 and 8.17, the cost of non-renewable energy like wind and solar has dropped exponentially since 1980, and that trend is projected to continue. If governments phased out subsidies to the fossil fuel industry, non-renewable prices would soon be at par with fossil fuels. An analysis from Bloomberg New Energy Finance compared the roughly $45 billion of global government subsidies for renewable energy to the $557 billion in subsidies for fossil fuels in 2008 alone.[14] That 12-to-1 ratio of dirty-to-clean subsidies is under pressure. People are asking why governments are subsidizing the most profitable industry in the world. The question becomes more pressing when we realize the $557 billion subsidy does not include billions of dollars the United States spends annually to ensure Persian Gulf shipping lanes are open for oil freighers, nor does it include the cost of the Iraq war, which Nobel Prize-winning economist Joseph Stiglitz estimates to be anywhere from $2.7 billion to $6 trillion. Feeding our addiction to oil is expensive.[15]

Eco-efficiency reduces dependency on energy from the grid. Generating renewable energy onsite mitigates energy price increases. Companies that are energy neutral, or close to it, are better positioned to weather tumultuous times and energy price volatility. As they reduce their energy use, they offset price increases. As they disconnect from the electrical and fuel grids, they buffer themselves from whatever happens to energy prices. That is sustainability at its best.

We very conservatively assume that the cost of traditional energy will rise by 10% over the next three to five years. We assume a 75% likelihood that these companies will see this increase in their energy expenses. That increase for Sam's Solutions and M&D Corp. is shown in Figures 8.14 and 8.15.

Taking action on energy consumption helps the company tread water on its energy expenses, which brings us to the next risk ...

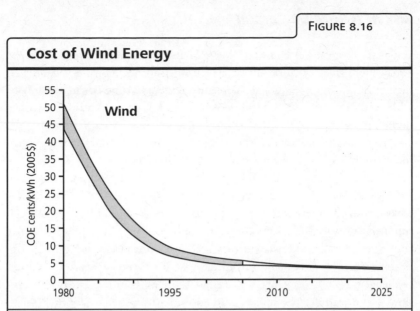

FIGURE 8.16

Cost of Wind Energy

Wind

COE cents/kWh (2005$)

Source: Adapted from "Renewable Energy Cost Trends (Levelized cost of energy [COE] in constant 2005$)" [accessed July 30, 2011], National Renewable Energy Lab Energy Analysis Office, November 2005. Available online at GENI.org.

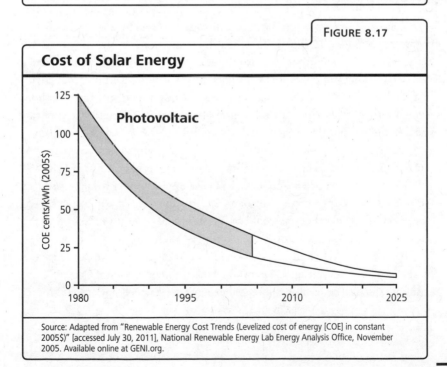

FIGURE 8.17

Cost of Solar Energy

Photovoltaic

COE cents/kWh (2005$)

Source: Adapted from "Renewable Energy Cost Trends (Levelized cost of energy [COE] in constant 2005$)" [accessed July 30, 2011], National Renewable Energy Lab Energy Analysis Office, November 2005. Available online at GENI.org.

Risk of a Price on Carbon

Ten years ago, carbon emissions and climate change were fringe concerns. Today, more than 3,000 organizations in 60 countries measure and disclose their greenhouse gas (GHG) emissions through the Carbon Disclosure Project, which acts on behalf of 551 institutional investors, holding $71 trillion in assets under management.

Pressure to reduce carbon is not easing up. In May 2011, the UK government announced an ambitious goal to slash GHG emissions by 50% by 2025 and unveiled 2030 and 2050 emissions-reduction targets of 60% and 80% below 1990 levels. The US General Services Administration (GSA), which purchases $500 billion of goods and services for all US federal agencies from 600,000 suppliers annually, is the largest procurer on the planet. As of July 2010, GSA contractors that did not track their GHG emissions risked losing their contracts.[16] Business customers increasingly ask for carbon footprint data and challenge carbon management policies. In 2009, Walmart requested CO_2 emissions data from 100,000 suppliers.[17] To minimize its carbon footprint, PepsiCo UK and Ireland's goal is to eliminate all fossil fuels from operations by 2023.[18]

In 2009, environmental researchers at Trucost analyzed the carbon intensity of the top 500 US companies listed in the S&P 500.[19] They found that, on average, companies emit 382 tons of carbon dioxide for every $1 million of revenue generated. Figure 8.18 shows the dramatic range of carbon intensity between sectors; Trucost found there are also significant differences among companies within the same sector. Corporate Knights' 2011 analysis of carbon productivity for the S&P/TSX 60 revealed an average of $3,361 of revenue per ton of carbon, which equates to 298 tons per $1 million of revenue.[20] We use 300 tons of carbon/$1 million of revenue as a rough rule of thumb for our sample companies.

Trucost also did some helpful calculations on companies' potential exposure if a price were to be put on carbon, assuming a price per ton of $28.24.[21] In October 2011, Australia announced a tax of $23 a ton that would take effect in mid-2012.[22] Depending on the particular business sector, the cost effects of a carbon price or carbon tax could be substantial. Figure 8.18 shows that the utilities and oil and gas sectors are the most exposed.

We conservatively assume a cost of $20 a ton for carbon and monetize the carbon risk by multiplying $20 per ton by the number of tons of CO_2 the company produces. The resulting potential expense for Sam's Solutions and M&D Corp. is shown in Figures 8.14 and 8.15.

FIGURE 8.18

Carbon Emissions by Sector in S&P 500

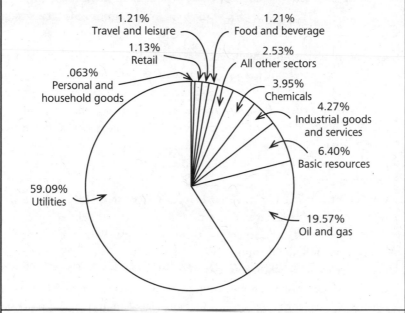

1.21%
Travel and leisure

1.21%
Food and beverage

1.13%
Retail

2.53%
All other sectors

.063%
Personal and
household goods

3.95%
Chemicals

4.27%
Industrial goods
and services

6.40%
Basic resources

59.09%
Utilities

19.57%
Oil and gas

Source: Adapted from Trucost "Carbon Risks and Opportunities in the S&P 500," produced for Investor Responsibility Research Center Institute, June 2009, p. 12.

Risk of Increased Cost of Waste

Could a company's cost of waste go up if it does not undertake aggressive efforts to reduce waste as part of its sustainability portfolio of initiatives? The answer is a resounding yes. The costs of each of the four contributors to the total cost of waste could rise. As described earlier, they are:

1. **Cost of materials purchased, but later wasted.** As we will see in the next section, there is a strong likelihood that materials will become more expensive in the next three to five years. Some resources are becoming scarcer, and it looks like the cost of fossil fuels used in their extraction, smelting, refining, and distribution will continue to rise as well. Since the cost of wasted materials makes up 60% of the total cost of waste, this is a significant contributor to the threat of higher costs if the company does not undertake a waste reduction program.

2. **Cost of processing the material before it is wasted.** This includes the wasted energy and labor used to work on the material before it becomes scrap. As discussed earlier, energy costs are likely to rise within the next three to five years. Judging by historic patterns, so will labor costs. This component represents 20% of the total cost of waste.

3. **Cost of waste prevention and environmental management.** The cost of personnel with formal environmental management responsibilities contributes 10% to the total waste cost. Sometimes overlooked is the informal help that "green teams" give to this waste prevention effort, as the Dow, 3M, and Interface examples in Figure 8.19 show. Companies that lack engaged employees may find employees are less committed to mitigating waste, making this a bigger challenge instead of a smaller one.

4. **Cost of end-of-pipe waste treatment and waste disposal.** Storage, haulage, disposal, tipping, and other fees for treatment and disposal contribute the last 10% to the cost of waste, and there is every sign that these costs will rise in the next three to five years. Historically, tipping fees rise by about 7% a year. In the United States, about 70% of solid waste goes to landfill, but more and more hazardous waste is banned from landfills; the number of landfills is shrinking, and their capacity is strained; and the trend toward privatizing landfills continues.[23]

So each of the four factors in the cost of waste is destined to continue to rise. We conservatively assume there is a 75% probability that the overall cost of waste will increase by 5% over the next three to five years. The resulting quantified expense risks for Sam's Solutions and M&D Corp. are shown in Figures 8.14 and 8.15.

FIGURE 8.19

Examples of Eco-Savings through Employee Engagement

Dow. Dow Chemical launched its Waste Reduction Always Pays (WRAP) program in the early 1980s. WRAP challenged employees to propose waste reduction initiatives offering greater than 100% return on investment (ROI) per year. In 1982, the first year, 27 projects met the standard, with a satisfying average ROI of 173%. The traction for the program continued to grow. In 1993, 11 years after the program began, the company adopted another 140 employee WRAP recommendations, with an average ROI of 298%. Over 10 years, Dow implemented 575 employee-suggested projects with an average ROI of 204% and audited cumulative savings of $110 million per year.

Source: Kenneth Nelson, "Dow's Energy/WRAP Contest, A 12-Yr Energy and Waste Reduction Success Story," *Proceedings from the Fifteenth National Industrial Energy Technology Conference, March 1993, Houston, Texas,* pp. 12, 13, and16.

3M. Through its voluntary Pollution Prevention Pays (3P) program, introduced in 1975, 3M reduced consumption of resources by preventing pollution up front — through product reformulation, process modification, equipment redesign, and recycling and reuse of waste materials. By 2011, 3M had implemented 8,100 employee suggestions with payback periods of under a year and saved over $1.4 billion, as well as eliminating over 3 billion pounds of waste.

Source: "3P — Pollution Prevention Pays" [accessed July 30, 2011], 3M.com.

Interface. Interface began its Quality Using Employee Suggestions and Teamwork (QUEST) program in 1995. It engaged cross-functional teams of about 15 associates each in identifying, measuring, and eliminating waste in its carpet tile manufacturing processes. As a result of their suggestions to minimize material usage and improve the efficiency of equipment and processes, QUEST had achieved a 50% reduction in waste cost per unit by 2011, resulting in $372 million in avoided waste costs.

Source: "Sustainable Carpets, Interface" [accessed July 30, 2011], GreenEconomyCoalition.org.

Risk of Higher Cost of Water and Materials

In the discussion of strategic risks, we accounted for the potential revenue a laggard company might lose if it had a poor reputation due to its water, material, and waste management practices. But such a company is not only exposed to a shrinking top line; it is also likely to experience escalating costs for its water and materials, which compounds the risk to the bottom line.

Up until now, we have not charged enough for water, so it has not caught our attention the way energy does. Many of us take it for granted. As a Canadian, I am embarrassed by the way we squander a precious natural resource. It is somewhat reassuring to see that I am part of the relatively insignificant "urban water management" wedge in Figure 8.20 — my water use is just a drop in the bucket of global use. However, by 2030, demand for water is projected to outstrip supply by 40%. The same year, at least half the world's population is likely to be living in areas of "high water stress."[24]

Prices for water worldwide rose 10% in 2010, well above inflation rates, and this trend is expected to continue.[25] Prices for materials are also on the rise, as represented by the trend line for the cost of copper shown in Figure 8.21. Escalating material costs are driven by two factors: their increasing scarcity, and the rising cost of oil that provides the energy to extract, refine, smelt, and transport raw materials before their productive use.

Earlier, we discussed four ways that companies on a sustainability journey can reduce their need for new raw materials and water. They can dematerialize their products and packaging — that is, use less material and water to produce a product of equal or better quality. They can substitute more plentiful material for scarce materials. They can separate, purify, and reuse materials and water onsite. Or they can create a closed-loop system in which they reclaim their products when the user is finished with them and remanufacture new products using the parts and materials in the returned products. These strategies enable companies to better control the price of their materials and water. The strategies also buffer them from price swings in the commodity market. None of these are easy to do, but the transformation pays off as the company becomes more independent of escalating material and water costs.

We very conservatively assume that costs of materials and water will rise by 5% within the next three to five years, without corresponding reductions in usage by the company. Given the trend lines on prices, we assume there is a 75% certainty of these price increases, resulting in the risk of expenses for Sam's Solutions and M&D Corp. rising as shown in Figures 8.14 and 8.15.

FIGURE 8.20

Global Water Use Is Increasing Sharply

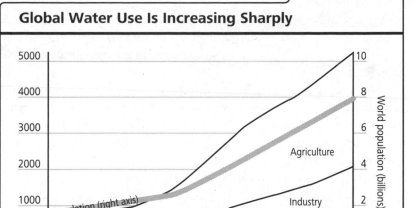

Source: Adapted from "Re-Engineering the DNA of the Capital Markets," Inflection Point Capital Management, July 2010, p. 3.

FIGURE 8.21

Cost of Copper

Copper

Source: Adapted from "Trends in the Costs of Raw Materials" [accessed July 30, 2011], TTIinc.com. Data from the London Metal Exchange.

Risk of Higher Cost of Capital

Managers should make environmental investments for the same reasons they make other investments: because they expect the new equipment or premises to deliver positive returns or reduce risks. Two good examples are described in Figure 8.22.

However, access to capital for any investment can be a challenge, especially in a time of tight credit. Lenders are increasing their requirements for loans and asking for more extensive disclosure about applicants' sustainability policies, management systems, track record, and stakeholder relationships to help them assess environmental and social risk. Why? First, environmental practices may expose borrowing firms to expensive legal, reputational, and regulatory risks that could jeopardize their solvency. Second, lenders want to ensure they are not stuck with the borrower's current and past environmental liabilities if the borrower defaults on the loan. Third, lenders are wary of risks to their own reputation if the public perceives they are abetting the borrower's irresponsible corporate behavior. For these reasons, laggard companies with poor sustainability track records may find they pay a higher rate for their borrowed capital.

In "Corporate Environmental Management and Credit Risk," the 2010 Moskowitz Prize–winning paper, the authors analyzed the environmental profiles of 582 US public companies and their associated cost of debt from 1996 to 2006 and recorded these findings:

- Companies with low environmental scores pay a premium for debt financing and have lower debt ratings from agencies like Moody's and S&P.
- Companies with better scores pay less for debt, but they tend not to be rewarded for their environmental performance by the ratings agencies. The agencies seem to lag individual bond investors regarding the significance of sustainability metrics.
- Perhaps most intriguing, the link between environmental risk and debt costs has strengthened. For example, bond investors seem to be pricing climate change–related credit risk in anticipation of laws yet to be passed.[26]

So the credit standing of borrowing firms is influenced by legal, reputational, and regulatory risks associated with environmental incidents. Companies with weak environmental performance pay a premium for debt financing, and companies with better scores pay less for debt. The spread can be as much as 64 basis points, and it is growing.[27] We conservatively assume that sustainable companies realize a 60 basis point reduction in the interest rate paid on their long-term debt. The resulting savings for our two sample companies are shown in Figures 8.14 and 8.15.

FIGURE 8.22

Sustainability Investments Pay Back

Marks and Spencer. M&S launched Plan A (described in Figure 6.12) in 2007, committing itself to address issues of climate change, waste, sustainable raw materials, "fair partnership," and health over five years. The company expected to invest £200 million in the program, but by 2009–10 Plan A had broken even and was adding £50 million to the bottom line. In response, M&S added another 80 commitments to the original 100 in Plan A.

Source: "How We Do Business Report 2010," Marks and Spencer, 2011, p. 3.

GE. General Electric spent $5 billion on R&D in the first five years of ecomagination, but the program to develop the clean technologies of the future generated revenues of $70 billion in that same period.

Source: "Ecomagination 2009 Annual Report" [accessed July 30, 2011], General Electric, 2010, p. 3, ecomagination.com.

Risk of Higher Voluntary Turnover and Lower Employee Productivity

There are three ways a poor track record on environmental and social responsibility could negatively affect productivity and talent retention: the firm could find that its talented employees drift away, that employees are away from the job more, or that employee productivity and innovation deteriorate.

First, voluntary attrition may rise. Over the last 15 years, a good CSR reputation has emerged as a critical retention factor — although a company's "greenness" is not the most important factor employees consider when deciding where they want to work, it has made the largest gains over other values, and its rapid rise suggests it may become even more important before long.[28] We conservatively assume that the voluntary attrition rate is 5% higher in companies with poor CSR reputations, and there is a 25% chance of this risk being realized. Figures 8.14 and 8.15 show the cost of this risk to Sam's Solutions and M&D Corp.

Second, employee productivity may decrease if the company does not proactively implement exemplary environmental, social, and governance policies and practices. Earlier, we considered how telework, teleconferencing, and video-conferencing improve employee productivity because time is not wasted on commuting or travelling. Employees working from home can more easily cope with the demands of child care, parental care, elder care for relatives, home maintenance, and overall family well-being, which mitigates stress.

Also, employees demotivated by a company's neglect of sustainability issues that concern them are less inclined to care about the company. Figure 8.23 shows that two of the three most critical factors in energy, materials, and waste saving programs are the engagement of staff and tenants. If they disconnect, technology solutions may be overshadowed by employee disinterest, which threatens eco-efficiency savings.

We assume that employee response to a company's poor sustainability efforts would be an overall increase in absenteeism, and a decrease in engagement, collaboration, and innovation. Our earlier calculation for the potential increase in overall employee productivity yielded a gain that was equivalent to 2% of the total salary for all employees. Without strong sustainability efforts, we conservatively assume there could be a loss of productivity equivalent to 1% of the total company payroll, and that there is a 10% probability of this happening. The potential increased costs for Sam's Solutions and M&D Corp. are shown in Figures 8.14 and 8.15.

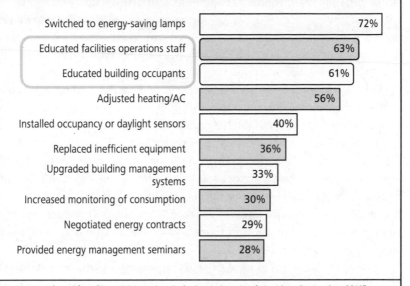

FIGURE 8.23

Top 10 Energy-Saving Actions

Action	Percentage
Switched to energy-saving lamps	72%
Educated facilities operations staff	63%
Educated building occupants	61%
Adjusted heating/AC	56%
Installed occupancy or daylight sensors	40%
Replaced inefficient equipment	36%
Upgraded building management systems	33%
Increased monitoring of consumption	30%
Negotiated energy contracts	29%
Provided energy management seminars	28%

Source: Adapted from "Top 10 Energy Cost-Reduction Actions, North American Corporations 2010" [accessed July 30, 2011], EnvironmentalLeader.com/charts. Based on Johnson Controls 2010 data.

Mitigating Compliance Risk

Companies must consider whether the potential impact of pending environmental and social regulations will be material. Fortunately, environmental enterprise resource planning (EERP) systems are available to help companies manage compliance and regulatory requirements. With a good EERP system, firms can quantify financial and economic risks from potential regulations and avoid higher insurance premiums.

One way to mitigate the impact of new environmental and social regulations is to be at the table when regulatory bodies draft them. Leaders in sustainability programs have earned that right. Laggards have not, so they may be blindsided by unexpected and intractable sustainability-related regulations.

A second way to mitigate the impact of compliance is to substitute environmentally friendly materials for hazardous substances like pesticides, dioxins, furans, CFCs, lead, and elemental chlorine before the regulations are enacted. It is usually less expensive to make the necessary changes voluntarily than to comply with more bureaucratic terms and conditions from unanticipated regulations.

A company occasionally must pay the cost of cleaning up accidental spills and releases, or cover fines and penalties. Most major companies pay for these costs from their operating budgets, but this expense could be mitigated by insuring against these spills. In February 2011, after five years of investigation and litigation, retailer Target agreed to pay $22.5 million to settle claims that it dumped hazardous and combustible liquids in local landfills for eight years.[29] In July 2011, a jury ordered Exxon Mobil to pay $1.5 billion in punitive damages for a leak of 26,000 gallons of gasoline from a Maryland gas station in 2006.[30] Legal costs in prolonged court battles and appeals often exceed the fine, especially if they have to contend with witnesses like the one portrayed in Figure 8.24.

Finally, forward-thinking companies can design closed-loop systems in which they take back their own products, and even those of competitors, instead of having users throw them away. Planning and implementing the logistics of product collection and disassembly can be cheaper than setting up such a system after it has been dictated by regulations.

Although the cost of the compliance risk could be substantial, we assume it is covered within the operational risk line items outlined in Figures 8.4 and 8.5, especially the ones associated with energy, materials, and water, so no additional risk is calculated.

FIGURE 8.24

Externalities Coming Home to Roost

"I get that it was wrong.
I don't get why it matters."

Source: Mike Baldwin, *Cornered* cartoon of June 29, 2010, gocomics.com/cornered.

Mitigating Financial/Stock Price Risk

If a company does not implement sustainability programs, do investors lose out? The Domini 400 Social Index, Dow Jones Sustainability Index, Sustainalytics' Jantzi Social Index (JSI), and the Financial Times (London) Stock Exchange Index all track companies rated as sustainability leaders. These indices perform as well as, or slightly better than, indices for the rest of the market, as shown in Figure 8.25, which compares JSI performance to that of the TSX 60. Sustainability leaders do not seem to sacrifice financial market value for their efforts, nor are others missing market gains.

Further, since 2000, academic researchers have conducted several meta-analyses and have found a small positive correlation between sustainability performance and financial/stock market results, and little evidence of a financial downside of having good or bad sustainability performance. In 2008, the Network for Business Sustainability commissioned Dr. John Peloza and Ron Yachnin to do a systematic review of thousands of studies from both academia and the corporate world on valuing sustainability. The two analyzed 159 studies and meta-studies published since 1972 and found that 63% showed a positive relationship between sustainability, which they call corporate social performance (CSP), and stock market performance, which they call corporate financial performance (CFP); only 15% of past studies showed a negative relationship.[31]

Still, methodological limitations of past research — such as over-reliance on old data and definitions, sampling problems, concerns about the reliability and validity of the CSP and CFP measures, lack of opportunities to test mediating mechanisms, and a need for a causal theory to link CSP and CFP — could result in either understatement or overstatement of findings.[32] Further research is needed, using more current data.

Intangibles/non-financials/reputation have become a larger part of a company's iceberg of market value in the last 30 years, as shown in Figure 8.26. Corporate attention to sustainability issues may be viewed as a proxy for good governance by financial analysts, but those analysts are still in the early stages of integrating sustainability considerations into their company valuations. Similarly, the increased weight of reputation in market capitalization may soon legitimize sustainability factors as valuation drivers. In the meantime, academic research and the performance of sustainability indices do not provide compelling quantitative support for a stock price benefit for good CSP, nor a risk of a CFP-downside for companies not embracing sustainability strategies. Therefore, we do not claim that sustainability strategies affect share price risks in our business case ... yet.

FIGURE 8.25

JSI vs. TSX 60, 2008-11

.JSI ■■■ TX60 ▨

Source: Adapted from "Sustainalytics Jantzi Social Index, Real Time Data" [accessed July 30, 2011], http://sustainalytics.com/real-time-data.

FIGURE 8.26

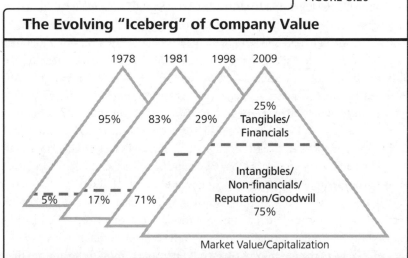

The Evolving "Iceberg" of Company Value

1978   1981   1998   2009

95%   83%   29%   25%
Tangibles/
Financials

Intangibles/
Non-financials/
Reputation/Goodwill
75%

5%   17%   71%

Market Value/Capitalization

Sources: For 2009, Hollender, Orgain, and Nunez, "The Business Case for Sustainability" [accessed July 30, 2011], Kaplan Eduneering/Seventh Generation Sustainability Institute, February 2010; for 1998 and 1981, Roberts, Keeble, and Brown, "The Business Case for Corporate Citizenship," Arthur D. Little, 2002, p. 1; for 1978, Stewart, "Accounting Gets Radical," *Fortune*, April 16, 2001.

Potential Burning Platform of Risks

Sometimes it takes a "burning platform" to trigger wholehearted endorsement of sustainability strategies. In *The Next Sustainability Wave*,[33] I relate how the "burning platform" expression came from a story told by Daryl Conner in *Managing at the Speed of Change*.[34] He described a nighttime explosion and fire on the Piper Alfa oil platform in the North Sea off the coast of Scotland on July 6, 1988. It was the worst catastrophe in 25 years of North Sea exploration: 167 people died, 61 survived. One of the survivors, Andy Mochan, leapt 150 feet (15 stories) into a burning sea of oil and debris, knowing he could survive only 20 minutes in the freezing water.

Why did Andy jump? When interviewed in the hospital later, he said he had chosen uncertain death over certain death — he knew that if he stayed in the inferno on the platform, he would die. The pain of the "status quo" was too great. He jumped because he had to, not because he was attracted by a personal growth opportunity. He was not trying to save the world; he was saving himself.

Personal and organizational change is often precipitated by a real or perceived "burning platform." The push of a risk or crisis is sometimes supplemented by the pull of the benefits that the change brings, but often the will to change is driven by discomfort with the status quo or unease about what might happen if a change is not undertaken. Fear is a powerful motivator.

So what is the burning platform of risks that could trigger corporate action on sustainability? We looked at how the company's revenue streams could be in jeopardy from a tarnished environmental and social reputation or an inability to win margin wars with competitors who capitalize on eco-efficiencies. We also considered how operational risks could blindside the company with higher expenses for energy, material, water, and financial capital. It may be poorly positioned to absorb the expense of internalizing carbon costs or externalized damage to ecosystems if/when those chickens come home to roost. It may find that talented employees, disillusioned by the company's lack of action on environmental and social issues that they care about, become less engaged and drift away to competitors. The status quo looks risky.

Figures 8.27 and 8.28 show how the summarized impacts of these risks flow through to the bottom line for Sam's Solutions and M&D Corp. The percentage of the revenue that normally flows through to the bottom line is used to size the percentage of the revenue loss that could negatively impact the bottom line. The platform is starting to smoke.

FIGURE 8.27

Sam's Solutions' Profit at Risk from Inaction

Strategic and Operational Risks	Annual Amount at Risk	Annual Profit Impact
Potential decreased revenue without sustainability initiatives	$51,500	−$3,605
Potential increased expenses without sustainability initiatives	$7,643	−$7,643
Potential impact of risks on bottom-line profits		−$11,248
Percentage of profits at risk		−16%

FIGURE 8.28

M&D Corp.'s Profit at Risk from Inaction

Strategic and Operational Risks	Annual Amount at Risk	Annual Profit Impact
Potential decreased revenue without sustainability initiatives	$25,750,000	−$1,802,500
Potential increased expenses without sustainability initiatives	$10,852,500	−$10,852,500
Potential impact of risks on bottom-line profits		−$12,655,000
Percentage of profits at risk		−36%

Conclusion

*Environmental problems are best analyzed as business problems.
Whether companies are attempting to differentiate their products, tie their
competitors' hands, reduce internal costs, manage risk, or even reinvent
their industry, the basic tasks do not change when the word "environment"
is included in the proposition ... Companies aren't in business to solve the
world's problems, nor should they be. After all, they have shareholders who
want to see a return on their investments. That's why managers need to
bring the environment back into the fold of business problems and
determine when it really pays to be green ... Imaginative and capable
managers who look at the environment as a business issue will find
that the universe of possibilities is greater than they ever realized.*

— Forest L. Reinhardt, "Bringing the Environment Down To Earth"

Potential Bottom-Line Benefits for M&D Corp.

We have carefully calculated the potential contribution each sustainability benefit could make to a more robust bottom line. The combined impact on M&D Corp.'s and Sam's Solutions' profits is shown in Figures 9.1A and 9.2A. The details behind the calculation are in the preceding chapters. By making explicit assumptions about the "so what?" of qualitative benefits like enhanced reputation or intrinsic motivation, we quantified their bottom-line impacts. Just as a standard business case would address both the upside of taking action to move toward Stage 4 or 5 on the five-stage sustainability journey and the downside of stalling at Stage 2 or 3, we show potential risks to profit from inaction, as well.

As in a standard profit-and-loss statement, not much top-line revenue finds its way to the bottom line. We assume that the current 7% ratio of profit to revenue applies to any additional revenue earned because of the company's sustainability efforts and enhanced reputation. On the other hand, 100% of the money saved through the five expense-saving benefits flows directly to the bottom line. That is why their contributions are so significant, relative to the contribution from revenue growth.

With such compelling potential profit improvements, it is reassuring that not all benefits are required. Some could be zero and the case would still be robust. Nor do all the benefit areas need to be pursued at once. Companies can focus on benefit areas with the fastest payback period first, prioritizing projects that yield the greatest energy, water, materials, and waste savings before the others. The results will build momentum, and some of the returns can finance other sustainability projects via the rotating Sustainability Capital Reserve, creating a multiplier effect. Further, although we assume that it takes three to five years for the potential profit improvement to be fully realized (also outlined in Figures 9.1B and 9.2B), aggressive action using best practices could accomplish the improvements in three or four years.

The range of 51% to 81% profit improvement for our two typical companies seems unrealistic. It is. It should be higher. Our biggest challenge has been to tune the assumptions so that the combined benefits yield a profit improvement of *less than 100%*. We have used cautious and conservative assumptions, and still the answer seems too good to be true. If the potential results are this good, why wouldn't all companies embrace more responsible environmental and social strategies?

Exactly.

FIGURE 9.1A

M&D Corp.'s Bottom-Line Profit Benefit

	Percentage Improvement in 3 to 5 Years	Annual Benefit	Annual Profit Increase
1. Increased revenue	9%	$45,000,000	$3,150,000
2. Reduced energy expenses	75%	$7,500,000	$7,500,000
3. Reduced waste expenses	20%	$7,500,000	$7,500,000
4. Reduced materials and water expenses	10%	$5,250,000	$5,250,000
5. Increased productivity and innovation	2%	$3,150,000	$3,150,000
6. Reduced employee turnover expenses	25%	$1,800,000	$1,800,000
Improvement in revenue and expenses		$70,200,000	
Impact on profit if sustainability strategies used	**81%**		**-$28,350,000**
Plus ...			
7. Avoided risks to revenue and expenses		$36,602,500	
Impact on profit without sustainability strategies	**–36%**		**–$12,655,000**
Plus ...			
Sustainability Capital Reserve, for more projects			**$12,750,000**

FIGURE 9.1B

M&D Corp.'s Five-Year Build to Full Benefits

	Percentage of Benefit	Annual Savings/ Improvements	Annual Profit Increase	Percentage Profit Increase
Year 1	30%	$21,060,000	$8,505,000	24%
Year 2	50%	$35,100,000	$14,175,000	41%
Year 3	70%	$49,140,000	$19,845,000	57%
Year 4	90%	$63,180,000	$25,515,000	73%
Year 5	100%	$70,200,000	$28,350,000	81%

Potential Bottom-Line Benefits for Sam's Solutions

Small and medium-sized enterprises (SMEs), also known as small and medium-sized businesses (SMBs), are important. Their aggregate environmental and societal impact is immense. What they lack in size they make up for in numbers.

Definitions vary between the European Union, the United States, and Canada but, in general, companies with fewer than 500 employees and less than $50 million in revenue are classified as SMEs.[1] Over 99% of the companies in all jurisdictions are medium-sized, small, or even micro (under 10 or 20 employees), and they employ 50% to 60% of the labor force.

What distinguishes SMEs from larger firms? First, their management structures and specialized positions are less well-defined and formal, so environmental and social responsibilities lie with busy staff people who have several other responsibilities. Second, cash flow trumps profit. A positive cash flow requires that a company be ruthless with ongoing expenses and minimize upfront costs required to reap benefits, so the business case focuses on benefits from early eco-efficiencies that have quick paybacks and short-term productivity improvements. Third, SMEs do not have the money, resources, or time to contend with environmental and social issues, and they cannot fall back on parent companies for expertise and support with funding. Fourth, SMEs often lump water, waste, and energy costs into "overhead" rather than tracking them in separate accounts, making it harder to identify and meter improvements.

On the other hand, SMEs are more likely to have local roots and to care about stewardship of the local environment and community, since that is where they, their children, relatives, and friends live. They are typically more intimately connected with their employees, investors, suppliers, and customers. They are more agile, and their shorter, less-bureaucratic decision chain allows them to respond quickly to changing market conditions. They can capitalize on the window of opportunity to reduce costs, improve sales, and stay ahead of the curve. When sustainability strategies are integrated within the overall business strategy in SMEs, they spawn innovative ways to achieve the benefits identified in the simulator and improve cash flow — just what SMEs want. Figure 9.2 shows the sustainability business case for a typical SME, Sam's Solutions.

FIGURE 9.2A

Sam's Solutions' Bottom-Line Profit Benefit

	Percentage Improvement in 3 to 5 Years	Annual Benefit	Annual Profit Increase
1. Increased revenue	9%	$90,000	$6,300
2. Reduced energy expenses	75%	$15,000	$15,000
3. Reduced waste expenses	20%	$2,500	$2,500
4. Reduced materials and water expenses	10%	$1,750	$1,750
5. Increased productivity and innovation	2%	$6,300	$6,300
6. Reduced employee turnover expenses	25%	$3,600	$3,600
Improvement in revenue and expenses		$119,150	
Impact on profit if sustainability strategies used	51%		$35,450
Plus ...			
7. Avoided risks to revenue and expenses		$59,143	
Impact on profit without sustainability strategies	–16%		-$11,248
Plus ...			
Sustainability Capital Reserve, for more projects			$4,250

FIGURE 9.2B

Sam's Solutions' Five-Year Build to Full Benefits

	Percentage of Benefit	Annual Savings/ Improvements	Annual Profit Increase	Percentage Profit Increase
Year 1	30%	$35,745	$10,635	15%
Year 2	50%	$59,575	$17,725	25%
Year 3	70%	$83,405	$24,815	35%
Year 4	90%	$107,235	$32,905	46%
Year 5	100%	$119,150	$35,450	51%

What's In It for Me (WII-FM)?

Executives understand the logic of the eco-efficiency benefits claimed for the generic companies Sam's Solutions and M&D Corp. throughout this book, but the resulting benefits, as shown in Figure 9.3, seem too large to be believable. These executives may suffer from a blend of the "NIH" syndrome, the "ten-dollar bill" syndrome, and other defensive mechanisms.

The Not-Invented-Here (NIH) syndrome inhibits adoption of good ideas from another company, especially a competitor. Admitting that another company's eco-efficiency innovation has value implies the home executive team was not smart enough to see it first, an uncomfortable admission for some. The "ten-dollar bill" syndrome is a corollary to this. It refers to the story of accountants carefully walking around ten-dollar bills lying on the floor because they assume that if the money were real, someone else would have already picked it up.[2] Some executives are so convinced they have already cleaned the economic floor that they are blinded to the remaining financial "litter" still waiting to be picked up. Learning requires a degree of humility.

But maybe executives' skepticism about the business case is less egocentric. Perhaps they think sustainability strategies are magical for other companies, somewhere else, in some other industry sector, some other time. Executives may be genuinely uncertain the results are possible for their company, in their location, in their industry, today. Understandably, they want to see the case for a company that is more like theirs than Sam's Solutions, M&D Corp., or the other sample hypothetical companies available in the Sustainability Advantage Simulator at sustainabilityadvantage.com. That's why the Sustainability Advantage Simulator invites them to plug their own numbers into the revenue, savings, and risk calculations. By adjusting the simulator's parameters according to their own experience and good judgment, executives can tune into WII-FM and learn the business benefits possible from aggressive strategies in their own company (see Figure 9.4). The business case is compelling for the sample companies — it may be for theirs, too. If executives still decide to ignore the possibilities, at least their decision is better informed.

The business case does not depend on new breakthrough technologies or new regulatory encouragements. Technological and regulatory progress would be helpful but is not required. Companies are already reaping the seven benefits using current technology in today's regulatory regimes. Attaining a sustainable borrow-use-return business model is not mission impossible. It is doable today, with significant gains on the bottom line. The only reason for delay is lack of leadership.

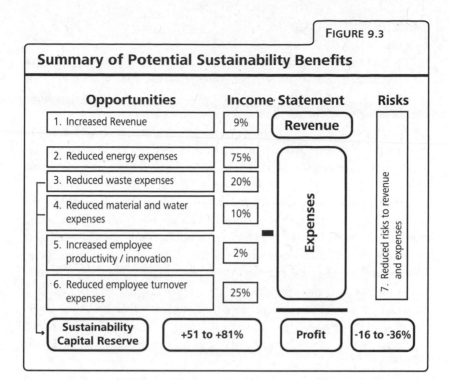

FIGURE 9.3

Summary of Potential Sustainability Benefits

Opportunities		Income Statement	Risks
1. Increased Revenue	9%	**Revenue**	
2. Reduced energy expenses	75%		
3. Reduced waste expenses	20%		
4. Reduced material and water expenses	10%	**Expenses**	7. Reduced risks to revenue and expenses
5. Increased employee productivity / innovation	2%		
6. Reduced employee turnover expenses	25%		
Sustainability Capital Reserve	+51 to +81%	**Profit**	-16 to -36%

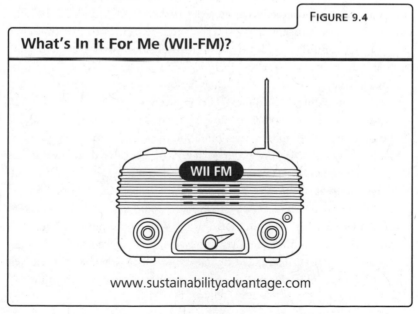

FIGURE 9.4

What's In It For Me (WII-FM)?

WII FM

www.sustainabilityadvantage.com

What about the Costs?

When I show audiences the enormous benefits that are possible when sustainability-related strategies are employed, they wait for the other shoe to drop. They want to know what the costs are in this cost-benefit analysis. Costs associated with sustainability initiatives are addressed in five ways.

First, funds for many sustainability efforts are already in line items in departments' operating budgets. Companies have budgets for communication, maintenance, advertising, and education. We are simply finding new ways to use those existing allocations, rather than suggesting that more money is required.

Second, sustainability projects requiring capital can be self-funded by the Sustainability Capital Reserve. We set aside half the savings from the reduced materials and waste benefits as a rotating pool of capital to fund sustainability projects. Many beneficial sustainability-related projects require amounts of capital too small to warrant C-suite attention. The Sustainability Capital Reserve can be used to cover those projects.

Third, companies can also take advantage of government grants and incentives for many sustainability projects. Early movers usually get the most grants.

Fourth, some capital projects may exceed the available funds in the Sustainability Capital Reserve, so they need to compete for the company's overall pot of available capital. Sustainability capital projects are approved the same way any capital project is approved. Companies only undertake capital projects that meet stringent payback periods and yield at least a minimum rate of return — the hurdle rate. If the capital has to be borrowed from an outside lending institution, loans for sustainability projects may receive a preferential rate, as explained previously. The business case assumes that the realization of the net benefits from sustainability-related projects is staggered over five years, as shown in Figures 9.1 and 9.2, to allow for various payback periods, so allowance for the impact of capital costs is built into the business case.

Fifth, many sustainability projects should be considered as investments rather than as costs. Other ways of enriching the bottom line pale in comparison to high-yield, low-risk investments in sustainability projects, especially when compared to how much more top-line revenue would have to be generated to have an equivalent impact, as illustrated by the Walmart example in Figure 9.5.

So we have allowed for the costs of sustainability projects five ways: business-as-usual expenses; self-funded capital projects; free grants and incentives; long-term loans at preferred rates; and high-yield investment opportunities.

FIGURE 9.5

Walmart Knows Savings Are Its Smartest Profit Booster

Walmart is investing aggressively: the $500 million it's putting into sustainability projects is projected to have a payback of four years or less and has become an incredible profit engine for the corporation. Begun in 2005, the initiative now saves more than US$500 million a year. Walmart works on three percent net profits, so to make another US$500 million in profit it would have to sell an additional US$16.7 billion in goods. Even for the largest retailer in the world, this would be a challenge.

Source: Jim Harris, "6 Surprising Green Tech Facts: What You Don't Know about Green Tech — But Should" [accessed July 30, 2011], Backbonemag.com, May 13, 2011.

Why the Business Case Is Hopeless

I love this Navajo proverb: "You can't wake a person who's pretending to be asleep." Corporations sometimes defend their inaction on social and environmental impacts by hiding behind Milton Friedman's adage that "The business of business is business." They claim that being more proactive on sustainability issues would violate their fiduciary duty to shareholders. Nice try. They are just pretending that they are unaware of the business case for sustainability or that it does not apply to them. With the potential benefits outlined above, maybe shareholders or investors should sue corporations if they *do not* integrate sustainability into their business strategies.

But why are they pretending to be asleep? Mindset. They are protecting their belief systems. "A man with conviction is a hard man to change. Tell him you disagree and he turns away. Show him facts or figures and he questions your sources. Appeal to logic and he fails to see your point." So wrote Stanford University psychologist Leon Festinger in the early 1950s, in a passage that might have been referring to the business case for sustainability today. A large number of psychological studies have shown that people use "motivated reasoning" to respond to scientific or technical evidence in ways that justify their pre-existing beliefs. People cherry-pick information that confirms what they believe, and reject data that does not.

Their entrenched mental models dismiss sustainability strategies as irrelevant to business. Sustainability seems like a future, abstract issue to some. To many executives, the words "green" or "environmental" may have a left-wing or anti-business connotation. Their mindset about environmental initiatives has been historically rooted in compliance issues, not productivity improvements or exciting new revenue streams, so it is no surprise that they tune out elements of the business case. Perhaps the "rapid escalation of complexity," which CEOs describe as their biggest challenge in the next five years (see Figure 9.6), will require them to take a new systems-level view of interrelated issues. A sustainability lens provides a helpful systems perspective and could be just the helpful rubric they need to rethink and simplify their business model.

There is a bestselling humorous bedtime storybook for children entitled *Go the F**k to Sleep!* It is tempting to write a companion bedtime storybook for hard-nosed business executives who are asleep to the potential benefits from sustainability-related strategies: *Wake the F**k Up!* Or perhaps we should acknowledge their deep-seated reasons for pretending to be asleep and help them *want* to wake up.

FIGURE 9.6

CEOs' #1 Challenge: The Complexity Gap

The CEOs' biggest challenge is the **rapid escalation of complexity.** 79% anticipate more complexity in the next five years; 50% doubt their ability to manage it.

IBM

Complexity drivers/Systems-level challenges

- Interconnected economies, enterprises, societies, and governments; more government regulations
- New economic environment: more volatile, uncertain, complex, and structurally different
- Global climate change
- Geopolitical issues surrounding energy and water supplies
- Vulnerabilities of supply chains for food, medicine, talent
- Sobering threats to global security

Source: "Capitalizing on Complexity," IBM CEO Survey, May 2010, pp. 13–21. Based on face-to-face interviews with 1,541 CEOs worldwide, November 2009 to January 2010.

Why the Business Case Is the Perfect Path to the Tipping Point

Traditional intuition blinds executives to the hard, bottom-line benefits that more than offset the costs of sustainable development. When the increased revenue opportunities, expense savings, workforce productivity and innovation gains, talent attraction and retention advantages, and risk avoidance benefits are monetized for smart executives, the light shines on a world of beneficial possibilities. The new way of framing the benefits around the opportunity-risk business case and income statement frameworks helps executives "get it" within the comforts of current decision-making methodologies.

Thomas L. Friedman, internationally renowned author, reporter, and columnist, says, "The way you get big change is by getting the big players to do the right things for the wrong reasons. If you wait for everyone to do the right thing for the right reason, you're going to be waiting a long, long time."[3] The business case for sustainability strategies supports moving to Stage 4 on the five-stage sustainability journey for bottom-line reasons. Some passionate sustainability champions feel this crass motivation sullies the cause. They need to understand that Stage 4 is a prerequisite platform for most companies before they choose to move to Stage 5 for the "right reasons" and re-charter their corporate purpose to legitimize enhancing social and environmental value as well as shareholder value. Those who are good at playing the game with today's rules earn the right to change the game.

As shown in Figure 9.7, when a critical mass — the right 20% of the big players — are in Stage 4 and/or Stage 5, we reach the tipping point at which sustainability will be quickly embedded within the core business strategies of most companies globally. The majority of CEOs believe that a sustainability tipping point will be reached within 10 years, as shown in Figure 9.8. We're getting close, and the radical hope for this business case for sustainability is that it will accelerate the pace.

Shrewd businesses will take the step to Stage 4, will be the successful leaders, and will thrive. As we have shown, the benefits are there for the taking. Executives who devote serious attention to using sustainability performance as a competitive weapon are well positioned to financially outperform their competitors in the 21st century. Smart executives grab the benefits before their competitors do. Companies that lag will be history, trapped in the hoax of an unsustainable business model. Companies that lead have the sustainability advantage.

FIGURE 9.7

Five-Stage Sustainability Journey

20%

5. Purpose/Passion
Align with founder's/CEO's values

- -

4. Integrated Strategy
Enhance company value/prosperity

3. Beyond Compliance
Save with eco-efficiencies
Avoid PR crisis
Avoid threat of new regulations

2. Compliance
Avoid fines, prosecution, bad PR

1. Pre-Compliance

Source: Based on Bob Willard, *The Sustainability Champion's Guidebook*, New Society Publishers, 2009, p. 11.

FIGURE 9.8

Time Until Sustainability Tipping Point

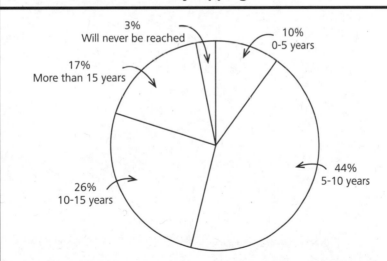

3%
Will never be reached

10%
0-5 years

17%
More than 15 years

44%
5-10 years

26%
10-15 years

Source: Adapted from Environmental Leader, "Time Until Sustainability Tipping Point is Reached, View of Global CEOs (% of respondents)" in *Environmental and Energy Data Book Q2 2011*, July 2011, p. 26. Based on UN Global Compact Annual Review 2010.

Notes

Bibliographical information for chapter opening quotes:

Introduction: Ray Anderson, *Confessions of a Radical Industrialist,* St. Martin's Press, 2009, pp. xiii–xiv.

Benefit 1: Andrew W. Savitz, *The Triple Bottom Line,* John Wiley and Sons, 2006, p. 22.

Benefit 2: Paul Hawken, Amory B. Lovins, and L. Hunter Lovins, "A Road Map for Natural Capitalism," *Harvard Business Review,* May/June 1999, p. 149. Reprinted by permission of *Harvard Business Review.* Copyright 1999 by Harvard Business School Publishing Corporation; all rights reserved.

Benefit 3: Ray Anderson, "More Happiness, Less Stuff" [accessed July 30, 2011], EnvironmentalLeader.com.

Benefit 4: Hawken, Lovins, and Lovins, "A Road Map for Natural Capitalism," p. 146. Reprinted by permission of *Harvard Business Review.* Copyright 1999 by Harvard Business School Publishing Corporation; all rights reserved.

Benefit 5: Chris Lazlo and Nadia Zhexembayeva, *Embedded Sustainability,* Greenleaf, 2011, p. 20. (The definition of an engaged employee is from Wikipedia.)

Benefit 6: Andrew S. Winston, *Green Recovery,* Harvard Business Press, 2009, pp. 142 and 161.

Benefit 7: Daniel C. Esty and Andrew S. Winston, *Green to Gold,* Yale University Press, 2006, pp. 116 and 117.

Conclusion: Forest L. Reinhardt, "Bringing the Environment Down To Earth," *Harvard Business Review,* July/August 1999, p. 157. Reprinted by permission of *Harvard Business Review.* Copyright 1999 by Harvard Business School Publishing Corporation; all rights reserved.

Introduction

1. WWF International in collaboration with the Global Footprint Network and the Zoological Society of London, "WWF Living Planet Report 2010," WWF Netherlands, 2010, p. 8.

2. The Natural Step, "The Four System Conditions" [accessed July 30, 2011], TheNaturalStep.org/the-system-conditions.

3. David Brower (1912–2000) was a mountaineer and environmentalist, first executive director of the Sierra Club, and founder of the Sierra Club Foundation, the John Muir Institute for Environmental Studies, Friends of the Earth, and the League of Conservation Voters.

4. Tim Jackson, *Prosperity Without Growth?* Sustainable Development Commission, 2009.
5. Richard Heinberg, *The End of Growth,* New Society Publishers, 2011.
6. United Nations Environment Programme (UNEP), *Decoupling Natural Resource Use and Environmental Impacts from Economic Growth,* UNEP, 2011.
7. Annie Leonard, *The Story of Stuff* video [accessed July 30, 2011], StoryofStuff.com.
8. According to the Bcorporation.net website, "Certified B Corporations are a new type of corporation which uses the power of business to solve social and environmental problems."
9. Aneel Karnani, "The Case against Corporate Social Responsibility," *Wall Street Journal,* August 23, 2010, online at WSJ.com.

Benefit 1: Increased Revenue and Market Share

1. "Ecomagination 2009 Annual Report" [accessed July 30, 2011], General Electric, 2010, ecomagination.com.
2. "Siemens to Generate Revenue of over €40 Billion with Green Technologies in 2014," press release, November 8, 2010 [accessed July 30, 2011], Siemens.co.uk.
3. Martin Bennett and Peter James, *The Green Bottom Line,* Greenleaf Publishing, 1998, p. 261.
4. "Ecomagination Fact Sheet" [accessed July 30, 2011], ecomagination.com.

Benefit 2: Reduced Energy Expenses

1. Paul Hawken, Amory B. Lovins, and L. Hunter Lovins, *Natural Capitalism,* Little, Brown, 1999, p. 53.
2. "Give Your Business Strategy a Jolt with the Deloitte reSources 2011 Study," Deloitte Center for Energy Solutions, 2011, p. 2. Available at deloitte.com.
3. "Green Building Facts" [accessed July 30, 2011], regreencorp.com.
4. Paul Hawken, "Natural Capitalism," *Mother Jones,* March/April 1997, p. 50.
5. Ernst Von Weizsäcker, Amory B. Lovins, and L. Hunter Lovins, *Factor Four,* Earthscan, 1997, pp. 10–12.
6. "TD Bank Opens Net-Zero Branch, Powered 100% by On-Site Solar" [accessed July 30, 2011], EnvironmentalLeader.com, May 13, 2011.
7. Von Weizsäcker, Lovins, and Lovins, *Factor Four,* pp. 20–29.
8. "Greening Your Business: A Guide to Getting Started," RBC Royal Bank, 2010, p. 13.
9. Jon Dee, *Small Business Big Opportunity,* Sensis Pty Ltd, 2010, p. 105. The book is available as a free download at about.sensis.com.au/small-business/free-sustainable-growth-book/.

10. Michael D. Barr, Chris Harty, and Jane Nero, "Enterprise PC Power Management Tools: Greening IT from the Top Down," QDI Strategies, 2010, pp. 2, 3, and 9.

11. Ted Samson, "Five PC Power Myths Debunked" [accessed July 30, 2011], CIO.com, December 11, 2008.

12. "Cloud Computing — The IT Solution for the 21st Century," Carbon Disclosure Project, 2011, p. 3.

13. "Shipping Fleet 'to Cut Emissions in Half'" [accessed July 30, 2011], EnvironmentalLeader.com, February 22, 2011.

14. "Department of Energy Seeks to Cut Solar Costs by 75 Percent" [accessed July 30, 2011], Reuters.com, February 4, 2011.

15. Paul Hawken, Amory B. Lovins, and L. Hunter Lovins, "A Road Map for Natural Capitalism," Harvard Business Review, May/June 1999, p. 156.

16. Ibid.

17. Ibid., p. 149.

18. Ibid., pp. 149–150.

19. Von Weizsäcker, Lovins, and Lovins, Factor Four, p. xx.

20. Hawken, Lovins, and Lovins, Natural Capitalism, p. 11.

Benefit 3: Reduced Waste Expenses

1. Environmental Management Accounting Procedures and Principles, United Nations Division for Sustainable Development, 2001, pp. 19 and 59.

2. Ibid., p. 27.

3. "Environmental Protection Expenditures in the Business Sector 2008," Statistics Canada, Catalogue no. 16F0006X, 2006, p. 6.

4. Environmental Management Accounting Procedures and Principles, p. 81.

5. Leslie Guevarra, "Lockheed Saves $2.6M in IT Energy Costs; Tops Water, Waste Targets" [accessed July 30, 2011], GreenBiz.com, April 20, 2011.

6. "Boeing 2011 Environment Report" [accessed July 30, 2011], boeing.com, June 2011.

7. Quoted in Carl Frankel, In Earth's Company, New Society Publishers, 1998, p. 172.

8. Brooke Farrell, "Debunking 6 Myths about the Materials in Your Company's Dumpster" [accessed July 30, 2011], EnvironmentalLeader.com, 2011.

9. "IBM Pioneers Process to Turn Waste into Solar Energy" [accessed July 30, 2011], zerowasteblog.recyclematch.com, August 12, 2009.

10. "GM Meets, Beats Landfill-Free Facilities Target" [accessed July 30, 2011], EnvironmentalLeader.com, December 14, 2010.

11. "USPS Makes $27m From Sustainability Efforts" [accessed July 30, 2011], EnvironmentalLeader.com, January 27, 2011.

12. "An Introduction to Eco-Industrial Networking and the Canadian Eco-Industrial Network," flyer from the Canadian Eco-Industrial Network, 2001, p. 2.

13. *Environmental Management Accounting Procedures and Principles,* p. 1.

14. Thomas Miner, "Pepsi's 'Path to Zero' Includes Eliminating All Fossil Fuels by 2023" [accessed July 30, 2011], SustainableLifeMedia.com, January 20, 2011, www.justmeans.com/blogs/Pepsis-Path-to-Zero-Includes-Eliminating-all-Fossil-Fuels-by-2023/427.html.

15. "Walmart Waste Program Diverts Over 80%, Expanding Nationwide" [accessed July 30, 2011], EnvironmentalLeader.com, March 18, 2011.

16. "GM Surpasses Landfill-Free Facilities Commitment" [accessed July 30, 2011], media.gm.com, December 13, 2010.

Benefit 4: Reduced Materials and Water Expenses

1. *"Environmental Management Accounting Procedures and Principles,"* United Nations Division for Sustainable Development, 2001, pp. 81 and 27.

2. Julian M. Allwood et al, "Going on a Metal Diet," WellMet2050 Project, University of Cambridge, February 2011, p. 3.

3. *Wikipedia,* s.v. "Recycling" [accessed July 30, 2011], en.wikipedia.org/wiki/Recycling#Costs.

4. Environment Canada, "Appendix I" in *Pollution Prevention Planning Handbook* [accessed July 30, 2011], 2009, www.ec.gc.ca/planp2-p2plan/default.asp?lang=En&n=56875F44-1

5. Ibid.

6. Adam Aston, "PepsiCo's Water-Saving Mission Flows beyond Its Factories" [accessed July 30, 2011], GreenBiz.com, April 19, 2011.

7. Carol Smith, "Voluntary Simplicity Lets Employees Give Themselves a Raise," *Seattle Post-Intelligencer,* May 22, 1998.

8. Ralph Reid, "Initiatives to Reduce Paper Use, Improve the Bottom Line" [accessed July 30, 2011], EnvironmentalLeader.com, January 11, 2011.

Benefit 5: Increased Employee Productivity

1. Nicholas Imparato and Oren Harari, *Jumping the Curve,* Jossey-Bass, 1994, pp. 57 and 58.

2. Daniel Pink, *Drive,* Riverhead Trade, 2009, pp. 83–145. See the excellent video, "Drive: The Surprising Truth about What Motivates Us," at youtube.com for a good summary of his book and findings, www.youtube.com/watch?v=u6XAPnuFjJc.

3. James Collins and Jerry Porras, *Built To Last,* HarperCollins, 1994, p. 94. Another paper provides proven practices for building sustainability into organizational DNA: Dr. Stephanie Bertels, "Embedding Sustainability

in Organizational Culture," Network for Business Sustainability, 2010. Available at nbs.net/.

4. "Driving Business Results through Continuous Engagement: 2008/2009 WorkUSA Survey Report," WatsonWyatt.com, p. 4.

5. "Survey Said!" [accessed July 30, 2011], Greenomics.ca, September 22, 2010, www.greenomics.ca/research/survey-said/.

6. Mitch Ditkoff, "Innovation from the Inside Out" [accessed July 30, 2011], CSRwire Talkback, April 21, 2011, csrwiretalkback.tumblr.com/post/4815191293/innovation-from-the-inside-out.

7. John Thackray, "Feedback for Real" [accessed July 30, 2011], *Gallup Management Journal*, gmj.gallup.com, March 15, 2001.

8. Deanne Dutton, "Allow Staff Time Off for Charity or 'Lose Them'" [accessed July 30, 2011], Telegraph.co.uk, April 28, 2011.

9. Chris Jarvis, "The Business Case for Employee Volunteering — Case #1" [accessed July 30, 2011], RealizedWorth.blogspot.com, June 16, 2011.

10. "Better Employees, Finances and Image: Why and How to Create a Corporate Volunteer Program — With Chris Jarvis" [accessed July 30, 2011], CauseCapitalism.com, April 8, 2010.

11. N. Plowman, "How to Control Employee Absenteeism in the Workplace" [accessed July 30, 2011], BrightHub.com, June 20, 2010, www.brighthub.com/office/entrepreneurs/articles/64682.aspx.

12. Kate Lister and Tom Hamish, "Workshifting Benefits: The Bottom Line" [accessed July 30, 2011], TeleworkResearchNetwork.com (TRN), May 2010, available at www.workshifting.com. The benefits are based on TRN's savings calculator, which assumes 50, 100, or 500 employees are teleworking half the time.

13. "Productivity" [accessed July 30, 2011], SuiteCommute.com, www.suitecommute.com/research-and-statistics/statistics/productivity/.

14. Verdantix, "The Carbon Management Strategic Priority," Carbon Disclosure Project, 2010, p. 10.

15. Paul Hawken, Amory B. Lovins, and L. Hunter Lovins, "A Road Map for Natural Capitalism," *Harvard Business Review*, May/June 1999, p. 153.

16. "The Dollars and Sense of Green Buildings 2006," Green Building Council, Australia, 2006, p. 5.

17. Joseph Romm, *Cool Companies*, Island Press, 1999, p. 98.

18. Hawken, Lovins, and Lovins. "A Road Map for Natural Capitalism," p. 149.

19. Gregory H. Kats, "Green Building Costs and Financial Benefits," Massachusetts Technology Collaborative, 2003, p. 6.

20. Marc Stoiber, "Green B2B: The Secret Sauce for Better Employees?" [accessed July 30, 2011], HuffingtonPost.com, January 24, 2011. Another white paper

provides good support for the value of employee education as a catalyst for employee engagement and company savings: "The Business Case for Environmental and Sustainability Employee Education," National Environmental Education Foundation, February 2010, neefusa.org/Business Env/.

21. Ibid.

22. James Grubel, "Australia's Carbon Tax Plan Passes Biggest Hurdle" [accessed October 31, 2011], Planet Ark, planetark.org/.

23. US Department of Labor, Bureau of Statistics, "Employer Costs for Employee Compensation — March 2011," press release, June 8, 2011.

24. "Average Annual Hours Actually Worked per Worker" [accessed July 30, 2011], Stats.OECD.org.

25. "Average Annual Wages — United States" [accessed July 30, 2011], Stats. OECD.org.

26. Rob Bauer and Daniel Hann, "Corporate Environmental Management and Credit Risk," December 23, 2010, p. 3. Available online at http://ssrn.com/abstract=1660470. Another paper confirms that firms with better CSR performance face fewer capital constraints: Beiting Cheng, Ioannis Ioannou, and George Serafeim, "Corporate Social Responsibility and Access to Finance," Harvard Business School, May, 18, 2011. Available online at http://hbswk.hbs.edu/item/6766.html. A third paper confirms that firms with better CSR scores experience a lower cost of capital: Sadok El Ghoula, Omrane Guedhamib, Chuck C. Y. Kwokb, and Dev R. Mishrac, "Does corporate social responsibility affect the cost of capital?" Journal of Banking and Finance, September 2011. Available online at responsiblebusiness.haas. berkeley.edu/.

Benefit 6: Reduced Hiring and Attrition Expenses

1. Matthew Guthridge, Asmus B. Komm, and Emily Lawson, "Making Talent a Strategic Priority," McKinsey Quarterly, January 2008, pp. 49–50.

2. Ram Nidumolu, C.K. Prahalad, and M.R. Rangaswami, "Why Sustainability Is Now the Key Driver of Innovation," Harvard Business Review, September 2009, pp. 57 and 64.

3. "8 Different ROI Aspects of Sustainability" [accessed July 30, 2011], CorporateClimate.net, July 31, 2010.

4. Deanne Dutton, "Allow Staff Time Off for Charity or 'Lose Them'" [accessed July 30, 2011], Telegraph.co.uk, April 28, 2011.

5. Derek Wong, "Top Talents Attracted to Socially Responsible Companies" [accessed July 30, 2011], EnvironmentalLeader.com, July 11, 2011.

6. Ibid.

7. Ann Bares, "2008 Turnover Rates by Industry" [accessed July 30, 2011], compforce.typepad.com/compensation_force/2009/03/2008-turnover-rates-by-industry.html.
8. Yves Lermusiaux, "Calculating the High Cost of Employee Turnover" [accessed July 30, 2011], TCIcanada.com, 2007.
9. "Potential Savings for Reducing Employee Turnover" [accessed July 30, 2011], Nobscot.com (based on public data from *Fortune Magazine*'s "100 Best Companies to Work For," January 2001).

Benefit 7: Reduced Strategic and Operational Risks

1. Verdantix, "The Carbon Management Strategic Priority," Carbon Disclosure Project, 2010, p. 7.
2. John Davies, "Corporate Water Strategies: All Watersheds Are Local" [accessed July 30, 2011], GreenBiz.com, June 12, 2011.
3. Ran Sanghera, "A Drought in Your Portfolio," EIRIS, June 2011, p. 1.
4. Ibid., p. 2.
5. Thomas Miner, "Pepsi's 'Path to Zero' Includes Eliminating All Fossil Fuels by 2023" [accessed July 30, 2011], SustainableLifeMedia.com, January 20, 2011.
6. Michael Taylor, "Greenpeace Accuses Barbie of Destroying Indonesia" [accessed July 30, 2011], PlanetArk.org, June 9, 2011.
7. Jonathan Bardelline, "SC Johnson Pledges to Use 100% Sustainable Palm Oil" [accessed July 30, 2011], GreenBiz.com, May 24, 2011.
8. Jonathan Bardelline, "Puma Reports $133M of GHG, Water Impacts in Environmental P&L" [accessed July 30, 2011], GreenBiz.com, May 27, 2011.
9. "World's Biggest Companies Cause $2.2 Trillion in Environmental Damage" [accessed July 30, 2011], EnvironmentalLeader.com, February 22, 2010.
10. Jackie Luan and Kusum L. Ailawadi, "Does Corporate Social Responsibility Build Customer Loyalty?" [accessed July 30, 2011], adage.com, May 24, 2011.
11. Ibid.
12. "Give Your Business Strategy a Jolt with the Deloitte reSources 2011 Study," Deloitte Center for Energy Solutions, 2011, p. 2, deloitte.com.
13. "2011 Energy Efficiency Indicator: Executive Summary," Institute for Building Efficiency, June 2010, p. 5.
14. Alex Morales, "Fossil Fuel Subsidies Are Twelve Times Renewables Support" [accessed July 30, 2011], Bloomberg.com, July 29, 2010.
15. Jim Harris, "6 Surprising Green Tech Facts: What You Don't Know about Green Tech — But Should" [accessed July 30, 2011], Backbonemag.com, May 13, 2011.
16. Tom Spoth, "GSA to Vendors: Go Green or Else" [accessed July 30, 2011], FederalTimes.com, July 12, 2010.

17. Verdantix, "The Carbon Management Strategic Priority," Carbon Disclosure Project, 2010, p. 7.
18. "2009/10 Environment Report" [accessed July 30, 2011], Pepsico.co.uk, January 2011.
19. Trucost "Carbon Risks and Opportunities in the S&P 500," produced for Investor Responsibility Research Center Institute, June 2009, p. 4.
20. "S&P/TSX60 Scorecard 2011" [accessed July 30, 2011], CorporateKnights.ca, June 2011.
21. Trucost "Carbon Risks and Opportunities in the S&P 500," p. 4.
22. James Grubel, "Australia's Carbon Tax Plan Passes Biggest Hurdle" [accessed October 31, 2011], Planet Ark, planetark.org/."
23. Edward W. Repa, "Solid Waste Disposal Trends" [accessed July 30, 2011], Waste360.com, April 1, 2000.
24. "CDP Water Disclosure" [accessed July 30, 2011], Carbon Disclosure Project, www.cdproject.net/en-US/Programmes/Pages/cdp-water-disclosure.aspx.
25. "Water — The Golden Opportunity for Business" [accessed July 30, 2011], GlobeNet.com, August 2010.
26. Rob Bauer and Daniel Hann, "Corporate Environmental Management and Credit Risk," December 23, 2010, p. 3. Available online at http://ssrn.com/abstract=1660470. Another paper confirms that firms with better CSR performance face fewer capital constraints: Beiting Cheng, Ioannis Ioannou, and George Serafeim, "Corporate Social Responsibility and Access to Finance," Harvard Business School, May, 18, 2011. Available online at http://hbswk.hbs.edu/item/6766.html. A third paper confirms that firms with better CSR scores experience a lower cost of capital: Sadok El Ghoula, Omrane Guedhamib, Chuck C. Y. Kwokb, and Dev R. Mishrac, "Does corporate social responsibility affect the cost of capital?" Journal of Banking and Finance, September 2011. Available online at responsiblebusiness.haas.berkeley.edu/.
27. Bauer and Hann, "Corporate Environmental Management and Credit Risk," p. 3.
28. Dr. John Izzo, "CSR and Employee Engagement: Does It Matter?" [accessed July 30, 2011], CSRwire Talkback, June 1, 2011, CSRwiretalkback.tumblr.com.
29. Jake Anderson, "Target to Pay $22.5M to Settle Toxic Waste Case" [accessed July 30, 2011], tcbmag.blogs.com, February 7, 2011.
30. Tom Hals, "Jury Says Exxon Must Pay $1.5 Billion For Leak" [accessed July 30, 2011], PlanetArk.org, July 4, 2011.
31. Dr. John Peloza and Ron Yachnin, "Valuing Business Sustainability: A Systematic Review," Research Network for Business Sustainability, 2008, p. 3, nbs.net.

32. Joshua D. Margolis and James P. Walsh, "Misery Loves Companies: Rethinking Social Initiatives by Business," *Administrative Science Quarterly* 48, no. 2, June 2003, pp. 274 and 278.

33. Bob Willard, *The Next Sustainability Wave*, New Society Publishers, 2005, p. 87.

34. Daryl Conner, *Managing at the Speed of Change*, Villard Books, 1993, p. 93.

Conclusion

1. "Small and medium-sized enterprises (SMEs): SME Definition" [accessed July 30, 2011], European Commission: Enterprise and Industry, ec.europa.eu.

2. Michael Porter and Claas van der Linde, "Green and Competitive: Ending the Stalemate," *Harvard Business Review on Business and the Environment*, reprint 95507 (originally published in *Harvard Business Review*, September/October 1995), p. 145.

3. Amanda Little, "Thomas Friedman Talks COP15, Mother Nature, and Father Greed" [accessed July 30, 2011], Grist.org, December 19, 2009.

Index

demands for supplier sustainability, 24, 40, 41, 132; green products, 42. *See also* supply chain

business-to-consumer (B2C) sector: green products, 42, 43; reputation, 10, 40, 46, 132–44, 146; sustainable brands, 40. *See also* customers

business travel, 108

C

Campbell's Soup, 58

Canadian Business for Social Responsibility (CBSR), 102

Canadian Tire, 52

carbon, 134, 136: cap-and-trade system, 62, 130, 134; cost of, 24, 148–49, 152; credits, 62, 63, 130; emissions, 24, 52, 54, 108, 153, 113. *See also* climate change; energy; fossil fuels

Carbon Disclosure Project, 41, 54, 108

carbon footprint, 24, 40, 59, 81, 132, 134

Children's Hunger Fund, 105

Chiquita, 56, 146, 147

Chrysler, 44

civil society, 4

climate change, 12, 134–35, 137, 179: affecting value chain, 146–47; cost of borrowing, 158; risks of, 144–45

closed-loop system, 18, 72, 78–79, 86–87, 88, 92, 138, 156, 162

cloud computing, 55

Coca-Cola, 136

co-generation, 57, 58

collaboration, 24, 86, 112–15, 117, 160

Collins, James, 96

combined heat and power (CHP), 57, 58

community relations, 18, 22, 41, 102–4, 144, 172

compliance risk, 130–31, 162–63

computers. *See* high-tech industry; information technology

Conner, Daryl, 166

consulting, 44, 45

consumables, 78, 90. *See also* materials

corporate governance, 10–11, 18, 20: and carbon reductions, 134; and employees, 102–6, 121-24, 160; socially and environmentally responsible, 24, 102–3, 164

corporate responsibility (CR), 10. *See also* sustainability strategies

corporate social responsibility (CSR), 10. *See also* sustainability strategies

cradle-to-cradle design, 78–79, 82, 86

customers, 30–31, 102–3, 146: align with sustainability values, 40, 42–43; debt, 16; employees as, 90; influence corporate decisions, 5, 83, 98–99, 134, 140; prices, 42, 56, 144; responsible consumption, 18, 40, 42–43, 119, 144; retention of, 28–29, 40, 138, 140, 144; social capital, 10. *See also* reputation; risks

D

debt: consumer, 16; corporate, cost of, 148–49, 158

Dell Computers, 54

Deloitte's reSources 2011 survey, 50, 150

dematerialization, 78, 79, 80–81, 156

design for disassembly (DfD), 86

digital technology. *See* high-tech industry

Dow Chemical, 44, 45, 155

by sustainable practices, 4–5, 14, 37–47, 170, 180 (*see also* leasing; green products); from new green products, 38, 42, 46; from new markets, 2, 3, 24, 29, 38, 42, 131; from onsite energy production, 57–59, 62, 71; relation to profits, 46, 62, 166, 170; risks to, 128, 132, 166–67 (*see also* strategic risks); in value chain, 30, 31; from waste, 68, 71, 72, 74, 90

risks: below the radar, 130; borrowing money, 158; categories, 130–31; climate change, 134–35; ecosystem damages, 142–43; increased expenses, 128, 148–63; materials management, 132–34, 136–39; as motivator, 128; to revenue/ profits, 128, 132, 166–67; of status quo, 166; suppliers or customers, 140–41. *See also specific categories* (strategic, operational, compliance, financial)

Robin, Vicki, 90

Rocky Mountain Institute, 52

Romm, Joseph, 110

S

Safeway, 132

Sam's Solutions. *See* services company; sample company

Savitz, Andrew, 37

SC Johnson, 140

service and flow economy, 18, 44

service companies: green products, 42–45; new revenue, 44, 45, 46; sample company, 34–35, 46–47, 62–63, 74–75, 78, 92–93, 114–16, 124–25, 133, 149, 167, 172–73; sustainability benefits, 32;

turnover rates, 124; use of materials, 78; wages and salaries, 116. *See also* leasing; product take-back

sewage costs, 88, 89

shipping, 56–57, 81, 146–47

Siemens, 42, 46

small and medium-sized enterprises (SMEs), 172

social capital, 10. *See also* reputation

social costs, 142, 144

social license to operate, 132, 146

solar energy, 57, 58, 150–51

Sprint, 87, 90

Stage 3 companies, 20–21, 24–26

Stage 4 companies, 22, 23, 180

Stage 5 companies, 22, 23, 180

stakeholders: driving sustainability, 5; vs shareholders, 28

Stiglitz, Joseph, 150

stock market, sustainability indices, 164. *See also* financial risk

Story of Stuff, 16

strategic risks, 130–47, 166–67

subsidies, for sustainability, 50, 58, 61, 150, 176

substitution, 78, 79, 82–83, 90, 156, 162

supply chain: B2B relations, 10, 102–3, 172; carbon footprint, 132, 134, 152; regulatory compliance, 2, 24, 132, 152; risks from, 127, 130, 132–33; risks to, 146–47, 179; risks to reputation from, 132–33, 140–42; sustainable procurement practices, 3, 5, 24, 40–41, 74, 132, 134, 152

Sustainability Advantage Simulator, xvi, xvii, 34, 174

Sustainability Capital Reserve, 74, 92, 170, 176

VeriGreen, 45
Victor, Peter, 14, 15
videoconferencing, 108
volunteerism, 98, 104–5, 106, 113, 122

W

Wackernagel, Mathis, 16, 17
wages and salaries, 116, 121
Walmart, 71, 74, 134, 140, 177:
   supplier survey, 40, 41, 132
Walt Disney, 140
waste, 65: cost of, 66–69, 74, 148–49;
   decreased by leasing products and
   services, 44, 45; definition, 66;
   electricity, 60; electronic, 87;
   employee engagement, 154–55,
   160–61; hazardous, 154; management, 138–39; paper, 90–91;
   process redesign, 18, 24, 70, 86,
   155; recycling/reusing, 71, 72, 78,
   79, 84 (see also product take-back);
   reduction, 18, 20, 70–71, 74;
   revenue from, 68, 71, 72, 74; risk
   from poor management, 132–33;
   separating from contaminants, 84;
   sewage, 88, 89; treatment/disposal
   of, 68, 69, 74; unsustainable, 12–13,
   16. See also landfills; materials
waste stream, 91
water: climate change, 145; cost of,
   88, 89, 92, 148–49, 156; green
   buildings, 111; industrial use, 88;
   management, 136–37; reducing
   use of, 77, 88–89, 92–93; use, 157.
   See also materials
weather events, 146–47. See also
   climate change
WellMet2050, 80
Weyerhaeuser, 90
wikis, 112

wildlife habitat protection, 68
Willard, Bob, 81
wind power, 57, 58, 150–51
Winston, Andrew, 119, 127
wood preservatives, 83
work from home. See telecommuting
working conditions: attract customers, 144; corporate reputation, 141;
   health and safety, 2, 9, 10; hours,
   116; in sustainable business, 18;
   regulatory compliance, 20–21;
   wages and salaries, 116, 121.
   See also employees
WorkUSA, 98
World Business Council for
   Sustainable Development, 142
World Resources Institute, 142

Y

Yachnin, Ron, 164

Z

Zhexembayeva, Nadia, 95

About the Author

Bob is a leading expert on quantifying and selling the business value of corporate sustainability strategies and has given hundreds of keynote presentations to corporate, government, university, and NGO audiences. Bob applies his business and leadership experience from his 34 year career at IBM Canada to engage the business community in proactively avoiding risks and capturing opportunities associated with environmental and social issues.

He has authored books, produced DVDs, created worksheets, and built an extensive slide set as capacity-building resources for champions of sustainability. They provide quantified business justification for embracing sustainability strategies and proven guidance on how to transform organizations to sustainable enterprises.

Bob serves on the advisory boards of The Natural Step Canada, Learning for a Sustainable Future, and Durham Sustain Ability. He is on ad hoc advisory committees for sustainable business certificate programs at Seneca College, Algonquin College, and Ryerson University, and is a member of the Durham Region Roundtable on Climate Change, and the International Society of Sustainability Professionals (ISSP). Bob is proud to be one of the five inaugural members of the ISSP Hall of Fame in 2011, along with Ray Anderson, Gil Friend, Amory Lovins, and Karl Henrik Robert. As of 2011, he is a certified B Corporation.

He has a BSc from McGill University (1964) and an MEd (2000) and PhD (2005) from the University of Toronto. Residents of Ontario, Bob and his wife are the proud parents of three adult children, the proud grandparents of three grandsons, and the proud owners of two hybrid cars: a Toyota Camry Hybrid and a Honda Civic Hybrid.

More information about Bob and his resources for sustainability champions can be found at sustainabilityadvantage.com.

If you have enjoyed *The New Sustainability Advantage,*
you might also enjoy other

BOOKS TO BUILD A NEW SOCIETY

Our books provide positive solutions for people who want to
make a difference. We specialize in:

**Sustainable Living • Green Building • Peak Oil
Renewable Energy • Environment & Economy
Natural Building & Appropriate Technology
Progressive Leadership • Resistance and Community
Educational & Parenting Resources**

New Society Publishers

ENVIRONMENTAL BENEFITS STATEMENT

New Society Publishers has chosen to produce this book on recycled paper made
with **100% post consumer waste,** processed chlorine free, and old growth free.

For every 5,000 books printed, New Society saves the following resources:[1]

23	Trees
2,120	Pounds of Solid Waste
2,333	Gallons of Water
3,043	Kilowatt Hours of Electricity
3,854	Pounds of Greenhouse Gases
17	Pounds of HAPs, VOCs, and AOX Combined
6	Cubic Yards of Landfill Space

[1]Environmental benefits are calculated based on research done by the Environmental Defense Fund
and other members of the Paper Task Force who study the environmental impacts of the paper
industry.

For a full list of NSP's titles, please call 1-800-567-6772 *or check out our website* at:

www.newsociety.com

NEW SOCIETY PUBLISHERS
Deep Green for over 30 years